HOW TO WRITE SHORT STORIES AND USE THEM TO FURTHER YOUR WRITING CAREER

JAMES SCOTT BELL

1

WHAT IS A SHORT STORY?

There's an episode of *Seinfeld* where Jerry goes to pick up a rental car. He'd reserved a certain model. But the agent at the counter says they don't have any of those models available.

Jerry protests, "But the reservation keeps the car here. That's why you have the reservation."

"I think I know why we have reservations," says the agent.

"I don't think you do," says Jerry. "If you did, I'd have a car. See, you know how to *take* the reservation, you just don't know how to *hold* the reservation. And that's really the most important part of the reservation–the holding."

Then, flailing his arms around, Jerry observes, "Anybody can just take 'em!"

Which brings us to the subject of short story writing.

(Cue flailing arms): Anybody can just type a bunch of words. The words can be about characters in a scene or two. The words may have a nice sound, too. And even add up to short-story length.

But that's not the most important part of a story.

The most important part is *emotional impact*.

On some level, you must move the reader. They are giving you their time, even if it's just long enough to read your story. The story has to stir, mangle, delight or somehow engage their emotions.

Which is no easy thing to accomplish.

In this book, I'm going to give you a key that will make it easier for you to do it.

This key, by the way, applies to any genre of short story, from literary to pulp; from stories appearing in the most prestigious journals to self-published tales sold on Amazon.

Once you grasp this concept, the writing of a great short story will be much less daunting.

You'll still have to work at it, of course. Great writing *is* hard work, and short stories are especially challenging.

I want to help you meet that challenge, and then suggest how you can use your short stories to further your writing career.

Short Stories Today

The early 20th century was a fertile time for the short story. At the turn of the century, writers like Jack London and O. Henry were wildly popular. At the same time, the market for pulp magazine content was exploding. Scores of writers whose names are virtually unknown to us today were cranking out short stories by the bushel for an insatiable reading public.

By the time the 1920s rolled around. you had two vast but wildly different markets open to you as a short story writer—literary and pulp.

The literary world was peopled with names like Fitzgerald and Hemingway, soon to be followed by the likes of Thomas Wolfe and William Saroyan. Their stories landed in prestigious magazines of the time like *Story* and *The Smart Set*.

Meanwhile, the pulp market (so called because these magazines were printed on cheap, wood-pulp paper, thus keeping the cover price modest) was seeing the rise of writers like Dashiell Hammett and Erle Stanley Gardner, followed by scribes such as Raymond Chandler and Robert E. Howard. Legendary pulp magazines included *Black Mask, Dime Detective, Amazing Stories* and *Weird Tales.*

After World War II, the pulp market began to dry up, leaving many prolific writers scrambling to find places to publish. Some writers moved to the "slicks." These were the magazines like *The Saturday Evening Post* and *Colliers,* printed on glossy paper, and having a large "middlebrow" subscriber base. (Another kind of slick came along in the 1950s, the brainchild of Mr. Hugh Hefner. *Playboy* did not rise to popularity because of its, er, reading material. But it did become one of the most important publishers of short fiction from the 1960s on. Alice K. Turner, the longtime fiction editor at *Playboy,* believed in the craft. She once made this observation: "If you're good enough, like Picasso, you can put noses and breasts wherever you like. But first you have to know where they belong.")

By the 2000s, there were fewer venues where you could place a short story. Slick magazines, falling to the disruption of online content, started to fold.

There were still publications like *Analog* and *Alfred Hitchcock's Mystery Magazine* for short genre works. And low-circulation journals like *The Iowa Review* and *AGNI,* for the literary set.

But the prolific short story writer became sort of like the Swaziland gnu—a rare breed.

And then along came a little something called the Kindle.

Suddenly, anyone could publish a short story in electronic form. They could even make a few bucks with it. But more important for the working writer, the e-story became a way to build up a readership for longer works.

When, that is, the stories are *good.*

About Emotional Impact

While there is some disagreement over the official length of a short story, a good rule of thumb is that it is between 1k and 7k words. Less than that and you get into the area of flash fiction. More than that and you move into the territory of the novelette (7k - 20k) or the novella (20k-50k).

The reason for this demarcation is that with increased length comes more complexity of plot and structure, and a greater range for multiple characters.

A short story, on the other hand, does quick work and then ends.

But quickness does not mean less emotional impact. Indeed, a great short story can have a punch every bit as memorable as a novel. It's all about getting the reader to *feel.*

As the great editor Sol Stein put it in *Stein on Writing,* the fiction writer's primary job is "creating *an emotional experience for the reader."* (emphasis Stein's). He compares the fiction writer to the conductor of an orchestra,

> his back to the audience, his face invisible, summoning the experience of music for the people he cannot see. The writer as conductor also gets to compose the music and play all of the instruments, a task less formidable than it seems. What it requires is the conscious practice of providing an extraordinary experience for the reader, who should be oblivious to the fact that he is seeing words on paper.

If there is no emotional experience, the work of fiction has failed. You may have a "message" you want to convey, but you would do well to remember the wise words of film director Frank Capra: "If you want to send a message, try Western Union." This from a man who made such "message" films as *Mr. Smith Goes to Washington* and *It's a Wonderful Life*.

Capra's great skill, of course, was "hiding" his message inside a film pulsating with great characters, plot twists, and emotion.

What kind of emotional impact, I must note, is variable.

An entertaining crime story with a twist ending, such as that written by Jeffery Deaver, leaves us with a happy snap, a feeling of being fooled and entertained.

On the other hand, a literary story about lovers growing apart by an Ernest Hemingway or an Irwin Shaw, makes us sad, holding a fictional mirror up to the tragedies of life.

And every other kind of emotion in between.

The choice is yours, but the goal is the same: If you want to write a great short story, you must create emotional impact. The stronger the better.

If only there was a key to guiding the writer on how to get there.

I believe there is.

Which is why I've written this book.

In college, I was able to get into a writing workshop led by one of the acknowledged masters of the short story, Raymond Carver. Each week a group of about fifteen students met in a classroom to work their stories. The big lesson I took away from that workshop was that I didn't have any literary talent.

What I mean is, I couldn't figure out *how* to write the kind of story Carver was known for. Or the kind that were being written by some of the students in that workshop. One fellow in particular seemed to have a natural gift at the literary short story.

I did not have such a gift.

Or, if I did, I wasn't able to find it.

Many years later, after discovering you could actually learn the craft of writing saleable fiction, and after having become a published novelist, I went back to thinking about the short story. I read and re-read some of my favorites. In various genres. All of Hemingway. All of Raymond Chandler. Most of Saroyan.

Raymond Carver, of course. And that other great Ray, Bradbury.

John Cheever.

Lawrence Block.

The stories in *Ellery Queen* and *Alfred Hitchcock*.

Stories literary, stories science fiction, stories crime.

And then one day it hit me, what the best of these stories had in common. I can't recall exactly how the thought occurred, but I started to test it.

And found that it worked.

I call this the *key*. Which I will discuss a couple of chapters ahead.

After we cover the structure of stories.

2

SHORT STORY STRUCTURE

There are, of course, differences between the structure of a full-length novel and the short story. Here are the fundamentals. Writers are free to stray from these guidelines. Just know that when you do, you risk losing the impact your short story might otherwise have. A short story that sticks close to these won't ever go wrong on the structural level.

Remember, story *loves* structure, because structure is what helps readers *get* the story you want to tell. You're doing readers a favor with structure. Play and experiment all you like. But when you revise, remember to think of the most important person in this exchange—the reader who is taking the time to read your story.

One Arc

The "feel" of a short story should be that it follows one trajectory, or arc. It concerns a character (or, in some cases, a group) heading through one primary crisis or concern.

In a novel, most writers adhere to a three-act structure.

Why? *Because it works every time. We seem to be structured ourselves —to receive stories that have a beginning, middle and end.*

A short story follows this pattern, too.

It starts somewhere.

It has a middle.

And it ends (somewhere short of 7k words).

The difference is in the complexity of plot. A novel can support subplots, multiple character points-of-view, and rich histories of setting. A short story cannot. It doesn't have time.

One Point of View

A short story almost always sticks to one point of view. Certainly, there's nothing illegal about incorporating another POV in a short story. Just know that when you do, the reader expects a full treatment of that character. This will begin to strain the story because it will want to push beyond its outer boundaries toward the novelette.

The point of view in a short story is usually one of three types:

First Person

I woke up with a screaming headache. Today was going to be one of those days.

Mary was still asleep when I got up to shower and shave.

Third Person

John Tanner woke up with a screaming headache. *Today was going to be one of those days,* he thought.

Mary was still asleep when he got up to shower and shave.

Omniscient

John and Mary Tanner were a happy couple. At least that's what they tried to project to people. Appearances were quite important to the Tanners.

One morning John woke up with a screaming headache.

While First and Third Person are close in terms of intimacy, Omniscient feels more distant. So why would a writer adopt this POV? In order to observe or comment on the action and characters, to be explicit or ironic in the telling. For example, the famous short story author Saki—real name Hector Hugh Munro (1870 – 1916)—has this section in the middle of his story "The Philanthropist and the Happy Cat":

The laws of tea-shop etiquette forbid that you should offer theatre tickets to a stranger without having first caught the stranger's eye. It is even better if you can ask to have a sugar basin passed to you, having previously concealed the fact that you have a large and well-filled sugar basin on your own table; this is not difficult to manage, as the printed menu is generally nearly as large as the table, and can be made to stand on end. Jocantha set to work hopefully; she had a long and rather high-pitched discussion with the waitress concerning alleged defects in an altogether blameless muffin...

Author voice is also evident in many of the stories by P. G. Wodehouse (1881 – 1975). In "When Doctors Disagree" we get this:

A number of eminent poets and essayists, in the course of the last few centuries, have recorded, in their several ways, their opinion that one can have too much of a good thing. The truth applies even to such a good thing as absence of jealousy. Little by little Maud began to grow uneasy. It began to come home to her that she preferred the old Arthur, of the scowl and the gnawed lip.

Raymond Chandler (1888 – 1959), perhaps the greatest stylist of hard-boiled detective fiction, demonstrates the use of author voice at the beginning of his short story, "Red Wind":

There was a desert wind blowing that night. It was one of those hot dry Santa Anas that come down through the mountain passes and curl your hair and make your nerves jump and your skin itch. On nights like that every booze party ends in a fight. Meek little wives feel the edge of the carving knife and study their husbands' necks.

It's clear that the use of author voice requires a unique style and definite narrative strategy. Give it a try sometime as a way to grow your author muscles. One of the reasons we write short stories is to develop a stronger prose style.

A note on tense: Almost always a short story is told in past tense form:

I walked down to the bank and saw Hank.

John walked down to the bank and saw Hank.

Past tense always works and is not jarring to the reader. But some writers like to try present tense on occasion:

I walk down to the bank and see Hank.

John walks down to the bank and sees Hank.

Present tense form calls a bit more attention to itself and requires a deft touch. So if you do use it, exercise caution, by which I mean don't let the style overwhelm the story.

Unless...

Unless you purposely intend to call attention to yourself. Which, if you do, it better be worth it to the reader.

Exposition and Backstory

Because a short story has limited space, some of the normal guidelines of novel-length fiction may be suspended for the sake of getting to the action.

For example, in a novel we usually try to avoid too much exposition or backstory in the opening pages. My usual rule of thumb for the novelist is *act first, explain later.* Readers will wait a long time for explanations if the novel opens with compelling characters and action.

In a short story, however, the writer may choose to front-load explanatory material. That way the reader is set up quickly for the heart of the story.

For example, Stephen King's story "Premium Harmony" begins this way:

> They've been married for ten years and for a long time everything was O.K.—swell—but now they argue. Now they argue quite a lot. It's really all the same argument. It has circularity. It is, Ray thinks, like a dog track. When they argue, they're like greyhounds chasing the mechanical rabbit. You go

past the same scenery time after time, but you don't see it. You see the rabbit.

He thinks it might be different if they'd had kids, but she couldn't. They finally got tested, and that's what the doctor said. It was her problem. A year or so after that, he bought her a dog, a Jack Russell she named Biznezz. She'd spell it for people who asked. She loves that dog, but now they argue anyway.

The first three lines cover ten years of marriage, and how it has devolved from "O.K." to "Now they argue quite a lot." Then King begins to put us in the Third Person POV (Ray) and a summary of his assessment of matters.

The second paragraph gives us more background in summary fashion.

The third paragraph begins the story proper, with a trip by Ray and his wife to Wal-Mart.

You'll find this type of opening in many short stories, contemporary and classic. It's a perfectly legitimate way to go. But also keep in mind you can start with the action (in medias res) and convey necessary information via dialogue. Jeffery Deaver does this in the opening of "Chapter and Verse" (included in this book):

"Reverend . . . can I call you 'Reverend'?"

The round, middle-aged man in the clerical collar smiled. "That works for me."

"I'm Detective Mike Silverman with the County Sheriff's Department."

Reverend Stanley Lansing nodded and examined the ID and badge that the nervously slim, salt-and-pepper–haired detective offered.

"Is something wrong?"

"Nothing involving you, sir. Not directly, I mean. Just hoping you might be able to help us with a situation we have."

So give good thought to the structure of your story. Before you write it, or after. As you plan, or as you look back over the text you have "pantsed." (The term *pants* refers to "writing by the seat of your pants," that is, without any plan at all.)

But by far the most important part of your story—the part that will spell its ultimate success—is in what I describe in the following chapter.

③

THE BIG KEY

"You must love the short story," writes Rick DeMarinis in *The Art & Craft of the Short Story,* "but you must also fear it."

Why would anyone say such a thing to a writer?

Because it's the truth. Short stories are daunting because they must do so much in so little time.

If they don't do much, why have them around?

We've already established that a short story needs to have emotional impact, and that the range of such impact is wide.

But is there one guiding principle which may be applied to all short story writing? A key that a writer can use to generate powerful short fiction every time out?

I think so. And here it is:

A great short story is about the fallout from one, shattering moment.

What is a "shattering moment"? Well, it's like when you shatter glass. You will never get the pieces together again. Something that was once whole and clear is no longer there.

It's a moment that changes someone's life, or at least their perspective on life. And afterwards, there is no going back to things as usual.

Now, understand that not all shattering is of the same force. If you throw a chair through a big bay window, that's a big kind of shattering.

But you can also drop a drinking glass on the floor. It's smaller, but it's shattered nonetheless.

If the story is not about one shattering moment (in ways we'll discuss in a moment), then I don't see how it even works as a story.

Perhaps someone will point to experimental forms of fiction. Thomas Wolfe, for example, tried different styles and methods over his career. But I would not call these attempts short stories. They are short experiments.

Experiments that did not work, in my humble opinion.

So unless your name is Thomas Wolfe and you live in the year 1935, another way to describe these short experiments is: *unpublishable*.

Or in other cases (I'm looking at you, Gertrude Stein) *unreadable*.

Test this definition for yourself. If you find a short story that has emotional impact without a shattering moment, congratulations. I have no idea what such a story would look like. So keep it on hand but also realize that it's an exception. If you can replicate the exception, have at it.

But also know that this key called the shattering moment will never let you down.

The Delivery of the Shattering Moment

All fiction writers are familiar with the admonition *Show, don't tell.* What it means in practice requires more explanatory space than is available in this book. Suffice to say for our purposes that it is more effective to create emotion in a reader *through the action of the story* than to tell the reader how a character feels.

John wept and pounded his fist on the table.

Works better than:

John felt really sad and frustrated.

As the great short story writer Anton Chekhov (1860 – 1904) put it: "Don't tell me the moon is shining; show me the glint of moonlight on broken glass."

So when it comes to rendering your shattering moment on the page, let the action of the characters reveal what's going on inside.

Action does not mean just the physical, but the verbal as well. Dialogue is a compression and extension of action—characters perform the act of speaking in order to further an agenda.

Thus, the shattering moment at the end of John Cheever's story "The Swimmer" occurs when the character, Ned, who has been "swimming across the county," arrives home.

The house was locked, and he thought that the stupid cook or the stupid maid must have locked the place up until he remembered that it had been some time since they had employed a maid or a cook. He shouted, pounded on the door, tried to force it with his shoulder, and then, looking in at the windows, saw that the place was empty.

On the other hand, the knockout blow is delivered via dialogue in Irwin Shaw's famous story, "Girls in Their Summer

Dresses." A middle-aged married couple are walking along Fifth Avenue in New York. The man keeps looking at nicely-dressed younger women, and the wife mildly complains.

Later, they go to a bar and order brandy. The wife keeps prodding the man to tell her why he keeps checking out other women. He tries to fend her off, but finally gives it to her:

> "When I think of New York City, I think of all the girls, the Jewish girls, the Italian girls, the Irish, Polack, Chinese, German, Negro, Spanish, Russian girls, all on parade in the city. I don't know whether it's something special with me or whether every man in the city walks around with the same feeling inside him, but I feel as though I'm at a picnic in this city. I like to sit near the women in the theaters, the famous beauties who've taken six hours to get ready and look it. And the young girls at the football games, with the red cheeks, and when the warm weather comes, the girls in their summer dresses ... " He finished his drink. "That's the story. You asked for it, remember. I can't help but look at them. I can't help but want them."

That's devastating to the wife, who is not like any of these women he has described.

Sometimes the shatter happens through the delivery of information. Many science fiction stories of the 1950s were of this type. For example, in "Common Denominator" by John D. MacDonald (1916 – 1986), an earthling gets a rather shocking bit of information from an advanced alien race on the subject of racial survival. What he does with that information when he returns to Earth is delivered in a terse, humorous form. The story is included in this book.

Finally, your shattering moment does not have to be negative. It can be a positive jolt, such as the sacrificial ending of O.

Henry's most famous story, "The Gift of the Magi." There the young couple each makes a sacrifice of something precious to them, because they love each other.

To sum up, the shattering moment is something that happens to a character, an emotional blast which they cannot ignore. It changes them, in a large or a subtle way—in a way that cannot be ignored.

Where Do You Place The Shattering Moment?

There are five places where the shattering moment can occur. The rest of your story will be shaped around this positioning.

The five places are:

1. The beginning of the story.
2. The middle of the story.
3. The end of the story.
4. Before the story begins.
5. After the story ends (the "implied" shatter).

Let's have a look at each.

1. The beginning of the story

In Lawrence Block's "A Candle for the Bag Lady," we begin with New York PI Matthew Scudder sitting in his usual haunt, Armstrong's bar on Ninth Avenue. A "thin young man in a blue pinstripe suit" enters the saloon looking for him.

The man joins Scudder at his table and explains that he's an attorney handling an estate. He informs Scudder that someone has died and left him the sum of twelve hundred dollars. The

name of the deceased is Mary Alice Redfield. Scudder doesn't
know who that is.

The attorney explains that the woman had been brutally
murdered—stabbed and strangled—and her body found in a
nearby alley.

Suddenly, it comes to Scudder. She was "the shopping
bag lady."

This news strikes him (the shattering moment). Why, he
wonders, would this woman have named him in her will? The
only contact he'd had with her was occasionally buying a newspaper from her. She would buy several from a newsstand then
set up her own "shop" in a doorway.

> I could remember a few occasions when I'd bought a paper and
> waved away change from a dollar bill. Bread upon the waters,
> perhaps, if that's what had moved her to leave me the money.

The legalities with the attorney are wrapped up and Scudder
is given a check for twelve hundred dollars. He puts it in
the bank.

> If Mary Alice thought I merited twelve hundred dollars, who
> was I to argue?
>   Ah, but it didn't quite work that way. Because somehow
> the money gnawed at me.

Notice that the money "gnawed" at him. That's how we
know this is the key to the story.

Scudder slips into a church. But his mind "didn't know
where to go."

> I stopped on the way out and lit a couple of candles for

various people who weren't alive anymore. One of them was for the bag lady. I didn't see how it could do her any good, but I couldn't imagine how it could harm her, either.

Now the remainder of the story is about how Scudder tries to track down the final days of Mary Alice Redfield.

The story ends when the mystery is solved. But it's not a "twist ending" (as discussed below). It's just the natural outcome of Scudder's quest. Which began with the shattering moment on the opening pages.

2. The middle of the story

Raymond Carver's story "Will You Please Be Quiet, Please?" is about a seemingly happy couple, Ralph and Marian Wyman. Married for eight years, two kids. During that time there had only been one "serious disturbance" in their marriage, something they hadn't ever really talked about. But the memory got to Ralph sometimes. A couple of years earlier, Ralph suspected that Marian had kissed another man at a party. And then he hit her.

And that's where they left it.

Now, as the story moves to the present, we open with the couple, seemingly happy. But then Marian mentions that party, and now Ralph wants to know exactly what happened, in detail. Marian doesn't want to tell. But Ralph pushes and pushes until Marian admits that it was much more than a kiss. It was, in fact, sexual.

That is the shattering moment and it's near the middle of the story.

Then suddenly, he knew. His mind buckled. *Cuckold*. For a moment he could only stare helplessly at his hands. Then he wanted to pass it off somehow, say it was all right, it was two years ago, adults, etc. He wanted to forgive. *I forgive you.* But he could not forgive. He couldn't forgive her this.

The rest of the story traces the emotional fallout of this revelation.

3. The end of the story

When the shattering moment occurs toward the end of the story, we are usually in the realm of the *plot twist.* Expectations have been set up. The reader follows along until ... *oh snap!* ... *I didn't see that coming!*

One of my favorite writers of this kind of story is Jeffery Deaver. I highly recommend his two collections of short stories, *Twisted* and *More Twisted* in which you'll find ample models of the surprise ending. One of my favorite Deaver stories is "Chapter and Verse," which is included in this book by the kind permission of the author.

When it works, a story of this type is extremely popular. But it's probably the hardest type of story to pull off.

Which makes the career of O. Henry so remarkable. Henry's real name was William Sydney Porter (1862 – 1910). At one point in his prolific career he was writing a short story every week for the *New York World Sunday Magazine.* These stories usually had the plot twist at the end, and were gobbled up by readers.

His story "The Last Leaf" is an example, and is included in this book.

Note that the shattering moment at the end doesn't have to be a genre-type twist. It can be an unexpected development that hits a character so hard that he or she ... well, shatters. See the ending of "The Swimmer," referenced above.

4. Before the story begins

Ernest Hemingway's justly famous short story, "Hills Like White Elephants," places the shattering moment before the story begins. What makes this even more remarkable is that the moment is never overtly explained. It is revealed in the dialogue, and when we figure out what it is, the emotional wallop is intensified.

The story begins with an unnamed couple sitting at a table outside a bar in Spain. They're waiting for a train to arrive. They order beer.

> The woman brought two glasses of beer and two felt pads. She put the felt pads and the beer glass on the table and looked at the man and the girl. The girl was looking off at the line of hills. They were white in the sun and the country was brown and dry.
>
> "They look like white elephants," she said.
>
> "I've never seen one," the man drank his beer.
>
> "No, you wouldn't have."
>
> "I might have," the man said. "Just because you say I wouldn't have doesn't prove anything."
>
> The girl looked at the bead curtain ...

There's obvious tension here. It comes through the dialogue and the subtle actions. But we still don't know why.

> The girl looked across at the hills. "They're lovely hills," she said. "They don't really look like white elephants. I just meant the coloring of their skin through the trees."
>
> "Should we have another drink?"
>
> "All right."
>
> The warm wind blew the bead curtain against the table.

"The beer's nice and cool," the man said.

"It's lovely," the girl said.

"It's really an awfully simple operation, Jig," the man said. "It's not really an operation at all."

The girl looked at the ground the table legs rested on.

"I know you wouldn't mind it, Jig. It's really not anything. It's just to let the air in."

The girl did not say anything.

Why has this guy suddenly changed the subject? What operation? Why isn't the girl answering? Why is she looking at the ground?

"I'll go with you and I'll stay with you all the time. They just let the air in and then it's all perfectly natural."

"Then what will we do afterwards?"

"We'll be fine afterwards. Just like we were before."

"What makes you think so?"

"That's the only thing that bothers us. It's the only thing that's made us unhappy."

The girl looked at the bead curtain ...

Now we know what happened before. The woman is pregnant; the man wants her to have an abortion. The word *abortion* is never used in the story.

You should read the whole thing to see how this plays out. Hemingway masterfully shows (not tells) how this shattering moment affects both of the characters, most likely forever.

A variation on this type of shatter is the *frame story*. That's a story that begins in the present then goes into an extended flashback—the story proper, where the moment occurs—and comes back to the present for the finish. My story "Golden" uses this device, and is included in this book.

5. After the story ends (the "implied" shatter)

John O'Hara (1905-1970) was one of America's most distin-guished short story writers. Though his literary reputation has long been in decline (probably due to literary scores being settled at his expense; he was a notoriously difficult person to work with), O'Hara's style was unique. As Charles McGrath put it in a *Time* magazine review some years ago, John O'Hara "cre-ated what later came to be called 'the New Yorker story'—one that turns on a tiny alteration in tone or mood—and he paved the way for Salinger, Cheever, Updike and even Carver."

O'Hara's short story "Everything Satisfactory" is set in Hollywood around 1946. Dan Schecter is a drinking man who shows up one night at the Klub Kilocycle at the corner of Hollywood and Sunset.

The next morning, Dan wakes up in his own bed, fully clothed. His car is in the driveway. How did he get there? He calls the headwaiter of the club, Paul, and asks what happened. Paul explains that he had another of the waiters drive him home and get him in the house. This is apparently not the first time. Dan Schecter is one of those Hollywood drunks who expects people to forgive him easily because of his charm, and who treats people pretty much like they owe him.

A few days later Dan goes back to the club and Paul greets him, as always. It's Paul's duty to make sure everything is satis-factory for Mr. Schecter. Dan's drink is double brandy and soda.

A singer, Mimi Walker, is performing. Dan asks Paul to have her join him for a drink after her set. Through the dialogue it appears Dan had come on to her once when he was drunk, and they may have had a tryst. Now Mimi isn't having any. "If you like the way I look, O.K.," she says, "but just don't start thinking of a return engagement."

When Mimi goes to join another table that asked to see her,

Dan stews and decides to wait. He keeps drinking. Paul keeps serving. The last few drinks have a little less soda in them. The subtle implication is that Paul is trying to get Dan good and stewed, and off Mimi.

Closing time comes around and Dan realizes he's alone in the joint. The story ends this way:

"Where's Miss Walker?"

"She went home, sir," said Paul.

"Where does she live? Foolish question number five thousand two hundred and eighty." He gulped his drink and reached in his pocket and took out a money clip. He put two twenties on the table. "I'll give you twenty dollars more if you tell me where—no, you wouldn't tell me, you son of a bitch." He stood up and staggered to the street. Paul came up behind him and said to the doorman, "Mr. Schecter's car."

In a moment or two a boy drove the car around from the parking lot, and Paul went back inside the Klub and leaned against the bar. Mimi was standing there, and they both watched Dan getting into the driver's seat. She was frowning.

"I can't let him go like that," she said.

"You stay where you are," said Paul. "We'll read about him in the papers." The car roared away.

Where is the shattering moment? It is implied that it will happen after the story ends. Paul, who had tired of Dan Schecter, was hoping Schecter would end up wrapping his car around a tree. Indeed, if Dan were to kick the bucket, it could even be murder.

It's left to our imagination.

This *New Yorker* type of story always has a subtle feel to it, of more going on beneath the surface. O'Hara was a master of dialogue, and that's where a lot of the emotional intensity of his stories are to be found—in the subtext of what people say, or don't say, to each other.

The Shattering Moment in a Humorous Short Story

In the case of a humorous story, such as was popularized by Mark Twain (1835-1910) and Stephen Leacock (1869-1944), the shattering moment still applies, but with a comedic caveat: the characters in the story must make something trivial of such importance that it becomes virtually a matter of life and death to them.

For example, take any *Seinfeld* episode. This was a "show about nothing." Of course, the things that seem nothing to us became of extreme and out-of-proportion importance to the characters.

Like the soup in "The Soup Nazi" episode. Jerry fell in love with the soup. So much so that when it came to choosing between the Soup Nazi (who ordered Jerry's girlfriend out of the store) and love, Jerry chooses the soup.

So in the humorous short story you find what it is that is driving the character to distraction, or interrupting his life, so much so that he'll be taken to places no normal person would be. And then you place the shatter anywhere you like, just as with any other short story.

For example, in Leacock's story, "Maddened by Mystery: or, The Defective Detective," you'll find a driven detective hot after clues ... as you gradually realize he's missing the obvious, which does not occur to him until close to the end. The hilariously absurd aftermath is one of the marks of a Leacock story. You can read it for yourself as it is included in this book.

4

HOW TO USE THE KEY TO WRITE A STORY

Now that we've covered the shattering moment and the five spots where it can occur, you can proceed to use it in any story you write.

Now, there are different approaches to the writing itself, as we all know. Some writers like to take off and write with just the spark of an idea. Ray Bradbury, one of our greatest short story writers, was this type. He would wake up in the morning and follow wherever his imagination led him. He once described this as "stepping on a landmine. The landmine is me." He then spent the latter part of the day "putting the pieces together."

This is an exciting way to write a short story. If you like this method, go for it! Write to discover what you're writing about. Then, at some point, brainstorm a shattering moment and decide where to put it!

Your story will suddenly show you what it means.

Another approach is to think up a shattering moment first. You can find one via character, event, setting, or theme:

.   .   .

Character: Let a character bubble up from your subconscious. Imagine the backstory of this character. Then create a current situation. Now ask yourself what will shatter this character's life? Where will you place that moment?

Event: Things happen to people. Car accidents, death, shootings, divorce, marriage, births, secrets revealed, secrets kept. Train your writer's mind to constantly be asking *What if?* Look around you, riff off the news, TV shows, overheard conversations. Your problem won't be how to get ideas; it will be how to choose which ones to write about. Pick an event and make it the shattering moment for a character. Now write a story around that.

Setting: Every setting you visit or read about has a potential story. Start with the world of your own work. John O'Hara often used Hollywood, where he lived and worked for a time, as a backdrop where any number of shady things can happen. Pick your setting, then let your imagination put people there. You know what to do next—shatter somebody.

Theme: Have you got something on your mind? Want to write out of anger or concern? Again citing Ray Bradbury, he wrote some of his science fiction not to predict the future, but to try to prevent it. The caution about writing from a theme is that your story can become didactic. You'll have to create characters who are not merely used as talking points. Be true to fully rounded characters. Give each side an argument. But find a place where you can shatter one of them. There's your story.

Story Starters

Short story writing improves your overall craft. It also works your imagination. A short story is like a wind sprint for the writer's mind. It will whip your creative vision into shape for the longer run of a novel.

Be on the lookout for story starters. There is a limitless universe out there of fiction stimulants. The more you look for them, the more receptive your imagination becomes. Here are a few suggestions to get you going.

Pictures

Images are everywhere: on billboards, the internet, print media. Give an image a moment of visual reflection and ask your mind to come up with a story idea.

Here's a photograph by Carol M. Highsmith, part of her public domain collection in the Library of Congress:

I posted this image on the writing blog, Kill Zone, and asked our readers to come up with an opening paragraph. You can view the results here.

. . .

The List

Begin today to make a list of nouns from your past. This was the famous practice of Ray Bradbury, and there's no better explanation of it than from the man himself. This is from his *Paris Review* interview, available online:

> I knew I had to dredge my subconscious, and the nouns did this. I learned this early on. Three things are in your head: First, everything you have experienced from the day of your birth until right now. Every single second, every single hour, every single day. Then, how you reacted to those events in the minute of their happening, whether they were disastrous or joyful. Those are two things you have in your mind to give you material. Then, separate from the living experiences are all the art experiences you've had, the things you've learned from other writers, artists, poets, film directors, and composers. So all of this is in your mind as a fabulous mulch and you have to bring it out. How do you do that? I did it by making lists of nouns and then asking, What does each noun mean? You can go and make up your own list right now and it would be different than mine. The night. The crickets. The train whistle. The basement. The attic. The tennis shoes. The fireworks. All these things are very personal. Then, when you get the list down, you begin to word-associate around it. You ask, Why did I put this word down? What does it mean to me? Why did I put this noun down and not some other word? Do this and you're on your way to being a good writer. You can't write for other people. You can't write for the left or the right, this religion or that religion, or this belief or that belief. You have to write the way you see things. I tell people, Make a list of ten things you hate and tear them down in a short story or poem. Make a list of ten things you love and celebrate

them. When I wrote Fahrenheit 451 I hated book burners and I loved libraries. So there you are.

The Dictionary

In addition to the nouns that come from your life, try opening a dictionary at random. Find the first noun you see and riff on it.

I just opened to: *beach buggy*, n., another term for dune buggy.

My riff:

Who would ride a beach buggy? A couple of guys with a couple of girls, and the beer is flowing. What if they roll over and one of them dies? What if they crash into a rich person's home? What if that rich person is a horror movie director and he locks them up? (Crime story)

What if it's an older couple on the dune buggy, reliving their past one last time? Is one of them dying? Alzheimer's? (Literary)

Two surfers on the dune buggy, seventeen, about to graduate. One of them shares a deep, dark secret. Murder? (Crime again!)

The News

Go to any of the online news sites. Or pick up an actual newspaper (while supplies last!). Read a random news item and ask yourself some questions:

- Who here has a shattering moment?
- Who isn't here who could have a shattering moment?

As I was preparing this book I went to the website of the

Arizona Republic and clicked on a local news story. Here's the headline and the opening:

It's National Chili Month! 10 restaurants for chili around Phoenix

It's the soup of the Southwest. And when temperatures in the desert (eventually decide) to dip, there are few dishes more comforting than a warming bowl of chili.

Although Arizona hasn't reached its pleasant temperatures yet, October is National Chili Month. So fill up those bowls on the chili of your choice — mild or spicy, with beans or not — at these 10

I ask some questions:

1. What if a restaurant owner and his wife have a fight over a chili recipe? What will that argument reveal about their marriage?

2. What if a crazy man takes over a restaurant with a gun, not for robbery, but for food?

3. What if a chili cook-off judge is being paid off? It's a small thing, but how does it affect him inside? How does that shatter his existence? Who can come along to catch him?

Of these three—which I jotted down quickly—I like the last one. It seems to offer the most originality as a concept, and good possibilities for exploring a character and finding out what makes him tick.

Prompts

There are many collections of writing prompts available to you. One such collection is from *Writer's Digest*—www.writersdigest.com/prompts—where you'll find hundreds of prompts like these:

- Ever since you were a child, you have burst into uncontrollable laughter every time you see a bare foot or bare feet. So far you've managed to suppress your hilarity at the sight of feet. Today, your boss has assigned you to cover the foot fashion show that is coming to town this weekend. The...
- You're a local disc jockey with a morning radio program. On your show you often take phone calls from commuters to talk about music and celebrity gossip, but on this particular morning you pick up a caller who says he's going to jump off the top of your building unless you play every song he...
- Write a story about three people who are on a road trip together, only to stop off at a gas station and pick up a fourth person whom they don't know. Why did they pick this person up? Where are they taking him/her? What happens?

First Line Game

I love a great opening line. Sometimes I'll just sit and write openings, without any thought of the novel or story to follow. First lines can be action, narration, dialogue—anything.

- She was waiting for the bus.
- "What are you doing here?" Jonathan asked.
- The Bottomleys seems like the nicest couple in the neighborhood.

When you do these exercises, remember: Don't over think. Let your mind play. Figure out what you have after you've written it.

Then shatter somebody!

5

PUBLISHING STRATEGIES

You have two primary options for getting your stories out to readers: You can submit them to a publication; or you can publish them yourself.

If you seek publication in a journal or magazine, the best way to research your options is via the annual *Novel & Short Story Writer's Market* (Writer's Digest Books). This comprehensive guide will tell you the best places to submit your type of story and what the guidelines are. There's also a section on contests. Winning a short story competition is something that looks good on a resume.

Short-form fiction published as independent, stand-alone works should not be viewed (at least initially) as a source of major self-publishing profits. That's because you have to price them at the lower end—99¢. At 99¢ the author receives just under 35¢ per sale.

There are a few prolific short story writers who argue for a $2.99 price point, even though they admit it will move fewer units and may even generate less income over time. For them, the value of their work on a story is reflected in that higher price.

The counter to this is two-fold.

First, short stories priced that high (unless authored by a Stephen King), almost always sit in the lower depths of Amazon—the "no discovery" zone.

Second, after several short stories are out you can create a collection and sell it at a higher price point and receive 70% of each sale.

Thus, my advice is that you not pin your hopes of self-publishing income solely on producing short fiction. Instead, use them strategically as described below.

The Kindle Select program

Kindle Select is a program Amazon offers under the Kindle Direct Publishing umbrella. By giving Amazon exclusive distribution rights (in 90-day increments), you can offer a work for free for five days. Those days can be spaced or used all at once. The other days in this period your story is priced as usual.

My preference is to use all five days in a row and get the word out on social media. The goal is to get eyeballs on the story and make new readers who will then want to seek out your full-length books. If you're just starting out and don't yet have full-length books, the free looks begin to build your readership for the future.

Free giveaways when people sign up for your email list

Successful indie writers know that the two best marketing tools are word of mouth, and an email list of readers. To start building that list, many authors offer on their blog or website a sign-up form which gives out a free story or book.

I recommend using at least a novelette-length story for this, and make it a good one. You not only want those sign-ups; you want readers who will become fans.

Serials

Many writers are now serializing their novels, using another model from the good old days. They'll publish in installments, with a low price. Some authors refer to this as episodic fiction, likening it to a television series such as *Lost* or *True Detective*.

Later, you can gather the series into one volume. But also listen to Hugh Howey's counsel: "I think it's a bad idea to simply chop up a novel into shorter pieces. Each work needs to satisfy on its own."

Howey emphasizes that each piece "should have its own beginning, middle and end. Cliffhangers only work if the protagonists have overcome some other obstacle along the way. Don't string your readers along; invite them back for more."

To promote a new novel

A few years ago the big publishing houses started commissioning short works from their A-list authors. Lee Child, Michael Connelly, and Janet Evanovich—just to name three—put out shorts featuring their popular series characters. This not only helped promote the next novel, but kept their readers engaged during that in-between period.

To keep your joy alive

Sometimes you need to write something just for the fun of it. This keeps your writing chops sharp and your writer's soul soaring. That's how it was with my short story "Golden." It's not my usual thriller or noir beat, but it was a story I needed to write. It makes me happy that it's out there—and that many readers have found it.

"If you like to read short stories, write them," Kristine Kathryn Rusch says. "It's that simple. Write what you love. That's really the most important thing—and believe it or not, the most important thing to making a living."

Lawrence Block, one of the grand masters of crime fiction, says much the same thing in *The Liar's Companion: A Field Guide for Fiction Writers:*

> I figured short stories would be fun. They always are. I think I probably enjoy them more than novels. When they go well, they provide almost immediate gratification. When they go horribly hopelessly wrong, so what? To discard a failed short story is to throw away the work of a handful of hours, perhaps a couple of days. In a short story I can try new things, play with new styles, and take unaccustomed risks. They're fun.

To increase your chances of success

If there's one consistent drumbeat from successful indie authors it is that production is essential. Not unlike that pulp era I talked about at the beginning of this book. For as one of the great pulp writers of the past, Edgar Rice Burroughs, once put it, "If you write one story, it may be bad; if you write a hundred, you have the odds in your favor."

Flash Fiction

The popularity of flash fiction (under 1k words) has grown enormously in recent years. There are numerous sites where you can read and publish flash. A simple internet search will reveal the venues.

The great value for the writer in doing some flash fiction is that it is like intense circuit training for the athlete. It makes you use plotting and characterization and editing muscles in a concentrated way. All that will benefit you when you get to work on other forms, including the novel.

Perhaps the most famous flash fiction is a six-word "story" that is often attributed to Ernest Hemingway. Supposedly Hemingway was lunching with some other writers at Luchow's, a famous eatery in New York's East Village. Hemingway boasted he could write a short story in only six words. After some harrumphs, Hemingway told the others to put a ten spot on the table.

He then wrote these words on a napkin: *For sale, baby shoes, never worn.*

The writers conceded Hemingway the money. (One argument in favor of Hemingway authorship is that his story, "Hills Like White Elephants," mentioned earlier in this book, has a similar theme).

Apocryphal or no, the emotional impact of this flash is evident.

Notice, too, it is about a shattering moment.

Have fun with flash and use it occasionally as a warm-up to your writing sessions.

6

HOW TO PUBLISH YOUR STORY ON THE KINDLE PLATFORM

Let's go over the basics of getting your short story published through Amazon's Kindle Select program. This means your story will be exclusive for the Kindle. You will not be able to publish it anywhere else. In return, you are getting placement in the Kindle store and access to five days of promotion when your story will be free.

Follow these steps:

1. Write and edit your story

Naturally. But do not overlook a freelance professional's proof read. You don't want any typos ruining the reading experience. I must admit that typos are like sand fleas—one or two always seem to slip in.

The nice thing about self-publishing is that if you hear from a reader, the typo is easy to fix in your source file for re-uploading to Amazon.

In addition to the story itself, be sure to include the

following in what's called "back matter" (any text that comes after the story ends).

Drop two spaces after your story ends and center either of the following:

The End

# # #

Then put in a friendly author note, inviting readers to know more about you by signing up for your email list. Here is what I have as the back matter for "Golden."

> Thank you for reading "Golden." If you would like to be notified when my new books and deals come out, you can sign up for my occasional updates HERE.
> For full-length books and other stories by me, please visit: http://www.jamesscottbell.com

The last item in my back matter is the copyright notice.

Copyright © [Year of publication] by [Your Author Name or Pen Name]
All Rights Reserved

2. Format it

It's easy to find an affordable freelance formatter who will prep your text for uploading to Amazon. The Kindle uses the .mobi ebook format. To get your story ready for publication, you can do one of the following:

Word

You can upload your Word doc or docx directly. Amazon, however, alerts you that this may result in a few odd formatting quirks.

Safer is to save your Word doc as HTML or "Web Page" (depending on your version of Word).

Scrivener

This amazing writing software does many things, not the least of which is the ability to compile a manuscript in different forms. One of these is .mobi.

Calibre

This is a free application that enables you to convert text into .mobi. There's a bit of a learning curve to it, but once you've got it down it's easy to get your stories Amazon-ready. Find it at calibre-ebook.com

Vellum

Vellum is a very sleek program for designing great looking ebooks (as of this writing, available only for Mac). It's a bit costly up front, but if you're planning to self-publish and format novel-length fiction, this could be a worthwhile investment. You can download the program for free to look it over. You'll be asked for a payment when you decide to use it for publishing. Go to: Vellum.pub

3. Create a cover

All authors know how important covers are in the browse-purchase cycle. Don't think you can get away with a "cheapie" look just because the story is a short one.

Which means unless you have the skill and the desire, don't design your own covers.

Instead, look for value-priced options.

A good place to start is with this comprehensive list provided by Joanna Penn:

http://www.thecreativepenn.com/bookcoverdesign/

You can create a distinct cover for each story, of course. But if you are going to be publishing several stories in the same genre, you might consider commissioning a template cover. This kind of cover keeps the same basic design, changing only the title, and perhaps one design element. That makes it easy for fans to know where a new story of yours fits.

4. Create your Kindle Direct Publishing account

If you don't already have one, create your own account with Kindle Direct Publishing (KDP). It's easy to do. You can set it up under your own name, or a business name (which will require some prep work before, such as a DBA, etc.)

Go to: kdp.amazon.com to begin.

5. Write the story description

All fiction offerings need a description, the "cover copy" that gives browsers an idea of what's in the story or novel. Since a short story is not as complex as a novel, the description can be simple. But simple does not mean dull! You want to whet the browser's appetite.

I suggest either one-sentence sizzle, or a 3-4 sentence description.

One Sentence Sizzle

You have a couple of options here: the direct approach, or the provocative question.

An example of the direct approach is the description for my story "Golden."

A game of catch between father and son brings back a memory that will change both their lives.

That's it. That's enough to convey the kind of story and a hint of what the tone is.

The provocative question approach is exemplified by Hugh Howey's "The Box."

What happens when artificial intelligence comes online, only to find itself locked in a room with a madman?

Simple. Effective.

Try several one-liners for your story. Test them on friends. You'll find the one that works best.

The 3-4 Sentence Description

The formula for this Is easy:

First sentence: Name the character(s) and his/her current situation or vocation.

Second sentence: the basic plot.

Third, the "story question." Another way to think about this is what's at stake?

Example: "No Time Left" by David Baldacci (thriller):

Frank Becker is a highly sought after, expert assassin. When Becker takes a mysterious job, he has no idea that it will force him to delve deeply into his own past. Undeterred by obstacles he is determined to complete his assignment. But he may realize too late that his success will permanently alter his future.

Example: "The Apartment" by Debbie Macomber (romance):

Hilary Sullivan's new apartment is the first place she's ever had on her own. She left San Francisco to live and work in Portland—and to get away from her much-loved but overprotective mother. Hilary's twenty-four, after all! But she soon discovers that the apartment comes with an unexpected roommate—Sean Cochran, a good-looking pilot who's just left the army and shows up at the place he thinks he's rented!

Work and re-work your story description until it shines. Your cover and your copy need to be the double-barreled inducement for the browser to click "Buy now."

5. Upload

You're ready to upload your story via KDP. The process is pretty intuitive. Just follow along and answer the questions (like, your name as the author!)

When it comes to choosing your categories, choose these two:

- FICTION > Short Stories
- FICTION > [Genre]

Next, you'll be able to choose seven "keywords" (which can actually be more than one word, separated by commas). These are additional tags that help browsers find titles that may interest them. Since "Golden" is a heart-wrenching father-son story, my keywords are: sons, boys, fatherhood, fathers, coming of age, feel-good, family love

Amazon itself offers these tips for choosing keywords:

Experiment .... Think like your customer. Think about how you would search for your book if you were a customer, and ask others to suggest keywords they would use.

Useful keyword types:

- Setting (Colonial America)
- Character types (single dad, veteran)
- Character roles (strong female lead)
- Plot themes (coming of age, forgiveness)
- Story tone (dystopian, feel-good)

Do NOT include the following in keywords:

- Information covered elsewhere in your book's metadata—title, contributor(s)
- Subjective claims about quality (e.g. "best")
- Statements that are only temporarily true ("new," "on sale," "available now")
- Information common to most items in the category ("book")
- Common misspellings
- Variants of spacing, punctuation, capitalization, and pluralization (both "80GB" and "80 GB", "computer" and "computers", etc.). The only exception is for words translated in more than one way, like "Mao Zedong" and "Mao Tse-tung," or "Hanukkah" and "Chanukah."
- Anything misrepresentative, such as the name of an author that is not associated with your book. This type of information can create a confusing customer experience and Kindle Direct Publishing has a zero tolerance policy for metadata that is meant to advertise, promote, or mislead.

- Quotation marks in search terms: Single words work better than phrases—and specific words work better than general words. If you enter "complex suspenseful whodunit," only people who type all of those words will find your book. You'll get better results if you enter this: complex suspenseful whodunit. Customers can search on any of those words and find your book.
- Amazon program names, such as "Kindle Unlimited" or "KDP Select"

You'll be prompted to upload your cover and your text.

Check the option "Do not enable digital rights management."

After the cover and story are up, go to "Preview Your Book." Have a look at it via their online previewer, to make sure it looks as it should. If there's a formatting error, you can fix it before publication.

Then you'll go to a new page for pricing.

Choose the 35% royalty and 0.99 USD price point.

Check the box that allows Kindle Book Lending. You want your story to go as far and wide as possible.

Click the box saying you agree to the terms of publication, then hit "Save and Publish."

And you're done.

When Amazon tells you your story is now available for purchase, go purchase it! Be the first sale. Start the snowball.

Now you can schedule your five days of free promotion. You do that through your KDP dashboard.

I recommend you use all five days at once, in a row (you can do this promotion every 90 days. Do it ... every 90 days).

For the promo, spread the word far and wide—to family, friends, social media. Get as many eyeballs on that story as you can.

Your story will default back to 99¢ after the promo.

Get to work on your next story!

A visual tutorial on uploading to Amazon may be found here:

https://www.youtube.com/watch?v=Tr6fPdj_QzE&feature=youtu.be

7

READING SHORT STORIES

Here are five of the stories mentioned in this book. There is a literary story ("Golden"), an uplifting story ("The Last Leaf"), a crime story ("Chapter and Verse"), a science-fiction story ("Common Denominator"), and a humorous story, ("Maddened by Mystery: or, The Defective Detective").

From now on, when you read a short story, look for the shattering moment.

If it isn't there, ask yourself if the story works. Or if it would work better if it had one.

Most of all, try your hand at writing short stories. You'll be the better writer for it. And deftly executed and published, they will certainly help you further your writing career.

Good luck!

"GOLDEN"

by James Scott Bell

We were at the park, Terry and I, when the dog ran up. Terry is my son, eight-years-old. I get him on alternate weekends. Mary and I reached an amicable settlement on custody, mainly because I didn't want to fight her anymore. Her family is well off and were not shy about retaining the biggest shark tank in L.A.

Me, I'm just plain old middle class. My old man was not present most of my life, and when he was he was usually tanked. Auto mechanic he was, and a darn good one. But in the machine shop of fatherhood he was all thumbs.

I was determined not to be that to Terry. I knew what I was in his eyes. The big-time athlete, the golden boy. Golden! Quarterback! Two years at Michigan. Drafted in the third round by the Eagles. I didn't make the squad and nobody picked me up. But my reputation got me into a partnership with a car dealership in my hometown of Woodland Hills, California.

Life was good there for awhile. I married Mary Canova (of the Encino Canovas, I always joked, but only partly. Her father's a big-time TV producer and her mother a former model who drips jewelry). We had Terry and I moved as gracefully into being a dad as I used to dance around the pocket as a Wolverine.

The dealership got going good, too. I had a steady clientele of folks who remembered me from Taft High, about a mile from Stenger's Ford on Ventura.

But then Mary had an affair, which I don't blame her for. I was working too hard and hanging out with some of my old buddies from Taft. I got into poker. The arguments with Mary got more heated. I doused my inner fire with bourbon. And I was too proud to give it up when Mary suggested AA.

We divorced when Terry was seven. I'd been sober for a year, but that didn't stop things. The hurt on Terry's face when we told him is a scar on my soul that will not heal. The only balm is when I'm with him.

Like this day, at the park, tossing the small football. Terry has good hands but I hope he doesn't take up the game. I want him to have two good knees and no concussions when he grows up.

Terry had just caught the ball when the dog ran up to him, jumping practically up to his head. It was a scruffy mutt, some middle-sized and exuberant breed.

Terry laughed and teased the dog by showing it the ball then throwing it to me.

The dog chased the ball.

Now it was my turn to laugh. As I threw the ball back to Terry, I saw the boy limping toward my son. He seemed to be a teenager, smallish. He wore jeans and canvas sneakers and a Lakers jersey with 24 on it. His limp and his constricted arm were pronounced.

"That's my dog," I heard him say in a nasally voice. "Sorry." He started walking away, calling his dog to follow him. I think the dog's name was Kobe.

Terry watched the boy for a moment, then looked at me and smirked.

That smirk was an ice pick through my heart. It cracked it open, and the memory of Charles and the dirt clod bled out and filled my chest.

His name was Charles August Whitmore. Never Chuck, or Charlie. Except to Robbie Winkleblack, who always called him Chaz the Spaz. I didn't call him anything, because he wasn't on my radar.

We were all seventh graders but not all of the same class, if you know what I mean. There were the guys who could play sports and the guys who couldn't. I was already big for my age and a three-sport guy—baseball, football, basketball.

Charles August Whitmore probably weighed eighty pounds if he was dripping wet and carrying a lunch box. His left arm was shorter than his right and his hand kind of curled up.

When we chose up sides, he was the pick nobody wanted. Mostly because he wasn't strong or fast and had a bum stick. But also because of his mouth.

Charles could take you apart with his tongue, which is what got him in bad with Robbie Winkleblack. Robbie called him Chaz the Spaz one day out on the field. Charles called him a "noxious emission."

When Robbie's face went blank, like he didn't know what Charles was saying, Charles said, "Don't you know the official name for a fart?"

That cost Charles one of the epic noogies of all time and the loss of his pants. Robbie got detention.

I was a witness, and I laughed. I laughed because Robbie was the only guy better than me out there on the field, and I wanted to be on his good side.

Which is part of the shame I carry to this day. But not as much as what happened after the dirt clod.

It was a Saturday, and Robbie and I played some basketball at the gym then went for a Slurpee. We walked back toward my house, taking the short cut over the hill.

The side of the hill was undeveloped then, and after a rain covered with long, wild grass. If you timed it right, if the dirt was just starting to harden, you could get yourself a monster dirt clod.

You did it by grabbing a bunch of grass and pulling up. A big old fist of dirt would cling to the roots. What you had then was a weapon, like a medieval flail. We used to twirl them around and throw them at each other.

This was a perfect day for a clod.

And something more.

A target.

Robbie was the first to spot him. "Isn't that Chaz the Spaz?"

He was looking down the hill. There was a house at the bottom with a new swimming pool. The pool didn't have water in it.

But it did have Charles August Whitmore, and he was running around. Making motorcycle sounds. He was a motorcycle in a motordrome inside his own little ESPN world. He had his arm out like he was holding handle bars. With his good hand he goosed the throttle.

"Think you can hit him?" Robbie said.

"With a dirt clod?"

"Yeah."

"He's too far away."

"Try it. I'll give you a buck if you hit him."

"And what if I miss?"

"You have to sing the USC fight song to me."

Robbie was a Trojan fan. I liked the Bruins.

"I don't have to hit him direct," I said. "Spray counts."

"No way, that's too easy."

"Chicken," I said.

"Dork," Robbie said. "Okay, go."

I grabbed myself some grass. The trick is not to yank too hard. And this one was a beauty. I wonder if there had ever been such a perfect clod before in the whole history of hills.

Charles was still making motorcycle sounds, running around that cement pool. I'm sure he thought he was going eighty miles an hour.

I took a step back and started twirling the dirt clod like some perverse David taking on a mini-Goliath. Countless dirt clod fights had perfected my technique. When I let go of the grass I knew it was going to land in that pool. The only question was how close to Charles it would come.

It couldn't have come any closer. Because the thing exploded right on top of Charles Whitmore's head. There was a puff of dirt smoke and Charles the Motorcycle stopped cold. He fell forward, tried to break the fall with his bad arm, and rolled down the side of the pool to the bottom.

And started wailing.

Robbie was already running away, laughing.

I ran away, too, but I wasn't laughing. I was thinking it was all over for me now. I'd be kicked out of school, maybe thrown into juvie.

When I caught up to Robbie he could hardly breathe, he was laughing so hard. "That was so awesome, bro!"

"I think he's hurt," I said.

"Bam! Right on his head! You are da man!"

"I mean really hurt."

Robbie said, "You're gonna be a legend."

"Shut up," I said. "Don't ever tell anybody."

"I gotta tell Tim and Josh. Come on, man."

"No," I said. "Shut up."

"Don't worry, bro. Legendary! That's you."

Charles was in school the next day. He had a bandage on his arm and there was a red welt under his blond hair that was easy to see if you were looking down on him.

I passed him in the hall and I remember him looking at me. I couldn't tell if he suspected anything. But there was fear in those eyes, that was for sure. Something got taken out of Charles in that swimming pool. In the gym, on the field, he didn't mouth off like he used to.

The school year ended in glory for me. We had an all-school flag football game. I went in at quarterback for the last half, we were down a score. I threw two touchdown passes, the last one in the final minute.

I got mobbed by my teammates and gym teacher Peter Furuta, who was our coach. As I was hugging Robbie I looked out into the crowd and saw Charles. He was smiling and clapping.

That summer my family went on a trip back east to see my great aunt. She wore heavy lipstick and liked to kiss me on the cheek. My dad took us—my mom, my sister and me—into New York for dinner and a Broadway show, *Annie Get Your Gun*. It was okay. Not as good as a Jets game.

When we got back to L.A., the first Saturday I went over to Robbie's house.

He was playing Sonic when I came into the living room and he stopped and said, "Man, did you hear about Chaz the Spaz?"

"No."

"Drowned."

"What?"

"Yeah, dude. I guess up at Big Bear Lake."

"How?"

Robbie shrugged. "Somebody said he was trying to swim to an island. At night."

"Why would he do that?"

Robbie shrugged again. Held up the joy stick.

I shook my head.

"Whattaya wanna do?" he said.

I don't remember doing anything with Robbie. I remember walking home. I remember walking by Charles August Whitmore's house. I remember being on the sidewalk and stopping to look at the house.

"Hello."

I turned and saw a woman there. She had hedge clippers and gardening gloves on. I knew right off it was Charles's mother. She looked just like him. Same build and face. She was tiny.

"Oh," I said. "Hi."

"Did you know Charles?" she said.

I nodded.

"You were in his class?"

I nodded.

"You look like an athlete."

I didn't do anything.

"Charles looked up to you boys. He really wanted to be—" Her voice choked off, like she'd cut it with the shears. She looked at the hedge she was clipping. She held the shears at her side. She breathed in and out.

There was a burning under my ribs. I wanted to do something, but knew there was nothing to be done. I'd not been near such grief before.

And something else. I couldn't analyze it. I didn't have the words or the ability to turn experience into understanding. Only later, much later looking back, was I able to find the word.

Self-loathing.

"I'm sorry," I said, as much for myself as for her. When her head did not move, I added, "He was nice."

"Yes," she said, and looked at the leaves as if they were tiny picture frames. "He was very, very nice."

Terry started limping toward me, imitating the boy with the dog. And smiling.

I shook my head at him.

His smile faded.

I got down on one knee.

He came to me then, not as the budding little man he wanted to be, but as a child wondering what he'd done wrong.

When he got to me I put my hands on his shoulders. Then I pulled him to me and held him. He couldn't have known what was coming next. He couldn't have known that gold was about to be tarnished.

But I will be his father.

"THE LAST LEAF"

by O. Henry
(Public Domain)

In a little district west of Washington Square the streets have
run crazy and broken themselves into small strips called
"places." These "places" make strange angles and curves. One
street crosses itself a time or two. An artist once discovered a
valuable possibility in this street. Suppose a collector with a bill
for paints, paper and canvas should, in traversing this route,
suddenly meet himself coming back, without a cent having
been paid on account!

So, to quaint old Greenwich Village the art people soon
came prowling, hunting for north windows and eighteenth-
century gables and Dutch attics and low rents. Then they
imported some pewter mugs and a chafing dish or two from
Sixth avenue, and became a "colony."

At the top of a squatty, three-story brick Sue and Johnsy had
their studio. "Johnsy" was familiar for Joanna. One was from
Maine; the other from California. They had met at the table

d'hote of an Eighth street "Delmonico's," and found their tastes in art, chicory salad and bishop sleeves so congenial that the joint studio resulted.

That was in May. In November a cold, unseen stranger, whom the doctors called Pneumonia, stalked about the colony, touching one here and there with his icy fingers. Over on the east side this ravager strode boldly, smiting his victims by scores, but his feet trod slowly through the maze of the narrow and moss-grown "places."

Mr. Pneumonia was not what you would call a chivalric old gentleman. A mite of a little woman with blood thinned by California zephyrs was hardly fair game for the red-fisted, short-breathed old duffer. But Johnsy he smote; and she lay, scarcely moving, on her painted iron bedstead, looking through the small Dutch window-panes at the blank side of the next brick house.

One morning the busy doctor invited Sue into the hallway with a shaggy, gray eyebrow.

"She has one chance in—let us say, ten," he said, as he shook down the mercury in his clinical thermometer. "And that chance is for her to want to live. This way people have of lining-up on the side of the undertaker makes the entire pharma-copeia look silly. Your little lady has made up her mind that she's not going to get well. Has she anything on her mind?"

"She—she wanted to paint the Bay of Naples some day," said Sue.

"Paint?—bosh! Has she anything on her mind worth thinking about twice—a man, for instance?"

"A man?" said Sue, with a jew's-harp twang in her voice. "Is a man worth—but, no, doctor; there is nothing of the kind."

"Well, it is the weakness, then," said the doctor. "I will do all that science, so far as it may filter through my efforts, can accomplish. But whenever my patient begins to count the carriages in her funeral procession I subtract 50 per cent. from the curative power of medicines. If you will get her to ask one question about the new winter styles in cloak sleeves I will promise you a one-in-five chance for her, instead of one in ten."

After the doctor had gone Sue went into the workroom and cried a Japanese napkin to a pulp. Then she swaggered into Johnsy's room with her drawing board, whistling ragtime.

Johnsy lay, scarcely making a ripple under the bedclothes, with her face toward the window. Sue stopped whistling, thinking she was asleep.

She arranged her board and began a pen-and-ink drawing to illustrate a magazine story. Young artists must pave their way to Art by drawing pictures for magazine stories that young authors write to pave their way to Literature.

As Sue was sketching a pair of elegant horseshow riding trousers and a monocle on the figure of the hero, an Idaho cowboy, she heard a low sound, several times repeated. She went quickly to the bedside.

Johnsy's eyes were open wide. She was looking out the window and counting—counting backward.

"Twelve," she said, and a little later "eleven;" and then "ten," and "nine;" and then "eight" and "seven," almost together.

Sue looked solicitously out the window. What was there to count? There was only a bare, dreary yard to be seen, and the blank side of the brick house twenty feet away. An old, old ivy vine, gnarled and decayed at the roots, climbed half way up the brick wall. The cold breath of autumn had stricken its leaves from the vine until its skeleton branches clung, almost bare, to the crumbling bricks.

"What is it, dear?" asked Sue.

"Six," said Johnsy, in almost a whisper. "They're falling faster now. Three days ago there were almost a hundred. It made my head ache to count them. But now it's easy. There goes another one. There are only five left now."

"Five what, dear. Tell your Sudie."

"Leaves. On the ivy vine. When the last one falls I must go, too. I've known that for three days. Didn't the doctor tell you?"

"Oh, I never heard of such nonsense," complained Sue, with magnificent scorn. "What have old ivy leaves to do with your getting well? And you used to love that vine so, you naughty girl. Don't be a goosey. Why, the doctor told me this morning that your chances for getting well real soon were—let's see exactly what he said—he said the chances were ten to one! Why, that's almost as good a chance as we have in New York when we ride on the street cars or walk past a new building. Try to take some broth now, and let Sudie go back to her drawing, so she can sell the editor man with it, and buy port wine for her sick child, and pork chops for her greedy self."

"You needn't get any more wine," said Johnsy, keeping her eyes fixed out the window. "There goes another. No, I don't want any broth. That leaves just four. I want to see the last one fall before it gets dark. Then I'll go, too."

"Johnsy, dear," said Sue, bending over her, "will you promise me to keep your eyes closed, and not look out the window until I am done working? I must hand those drawings in by to-morrow. I need the light, or I would draw the shade down."

"Couldn't you draw in the other room?" asked Johnsy, coldly.

"I'd rather be here by you," said Sue. "Besides I don't want you to keep looking at those silly ivy leaves."

"Tell me as soon as you have finished," said Johnsy, closing her eyes, and lying white and still as a fallen statue, "because I want to see the last one fall. I'm tired of waiting. I'm tired of thinking. I want to turn loose my hold on everything, and go sailing down, down, just like one of those poor, tired leaves."

"Try to sleep," said Sue. "I must call Behrman up to be my

model for the old hermit miner. I'll not be gone a minute. Don't try to move 'till I come back."

Old Behrman was a painter who lived on the ground floor beneath them. He was past sixty and had a Michael Angelo's Moses beard curling down from the head of a satyr along the body of an imp. Behrman was a failure in art. Forty years he had wielded the brush without getting near enough to touch the hem of his Mistress's robe. He had been always about to paint a masterpiece, but had never yet begun it. For several years he had painted nothing except now and then a daub in the line of commerce or advertising. He earned a little by serving as a model to those young artists in the colony who could not pay the price of a professional. He drank gin to excess, and still talked of his coming masterpiece. For the rest he was a fierce little old man, who scoffed terribly at softness in any one, and who regarded himself as especial mastiff-in-waiting to protect the two young artists in the studio above.

Sue found Behrman smelling strongly of juniper berries in his dimly lighted den below. In one corner was a blank canvas on an easel that had been waiting there for twenty-five years to receive the first line of the masterpiece. She told him of Johnsy's fancy, and how she feared she would, indeed, light and fragile as a leaf herself, float away when her slight hold upon the world grew weaker.

Old Behrman, with his red eyes, plainly streaming, shouted his contempt and derision for such idiotic imaginings.

"Vass!" he cried. "Is dere people in de world mit der foolishness to die because leafs dey drop off from a confounded vine? I haf not heard of such a thing. No, I will not bose as a model for your fool hermit-dunderhead. Vy do you allow dot silly pusiness to come in der prain of her? Ach, dot poor lettle Miss Johnsy."

"She is very ill and weak," said Sue, "and the fever has left her mind morbid and full of strange fancies. Very well, Mr.

Behrman, if you do not care to pose for me, you needn't. But I think you are a horrid old—old flibbertigibbet."

"You are just like a woman!" yelled Behrman. "Who said I will not bose? Go on. I come mit you. For half an hour I haf peen trying to say dot I am ready to bose. Gott! dis is not any blace in which one so goot as Miss Yohnsy shall lie sick. Some day I vill baint a masterpiece, and ve shall all go away. Gott! yes."

Johnsy was sleeping when they went upstairs. Sue pulled the shade down to the window-sill, and motioned Behrman into the other room. In there they peered out the window fearfully at the ivy vine. Then they looked at each other for a moment without speaking. A persistent, cold rain was falling, mingled with snow. Behrman, in his old blue shirt, took his seat as the hermit-miner on an upturned kettle for a rock.

When Sue awoke from an hour's sleep the next morning she found Johnsy with dull, wide-open eyes staring at the drawn green shade.

"Pull it up; I want to see," she ordered, in a whisper.

Wearily Sue obeyed.

But, lo! after the beating rain and fierce gusts of wind that had endured through the livelong night, there yet stood out against the brick wall one ivy leaf. It was the last on the vine. Still dark green near its stem, but with its serrated edges tinted with the yellow of dissolution and decay, it hung bravely from a branch some twenty feet above the ground.

"It is the last one," said Johnsy. "I thought it would surely fall during the night. I heard the wind. It will fall to-day, and I shall die at the same time."

"Dear, dear!" said Sue, leaning her worn face down to the pillow, "think of me, if you won't think of yourself. What would I do?"

But Johnsy did not answer. The lonesomest thing in all the

world is a soul when it is making ready to go on its mysterious, far journey. The fancy seemed to possess her more strongly as one by one the ties that bound her to friendship and to earth were loosed.

The day wore away, and even through the twilight they could see the lone ivy leaf clinging to its stem against the wall. And then, with the coming of the night the north wind was again loosed, while the rain still beat against the windows and pattered down from the low Dutch eaves.

When it was light enough Johnsy, the merciless, commanded that the shade be raised.

The ivy leaf was still there.

Johnsy lay for a long time looking at it. And then she called to Sue, who was stirring her chicken broth over the gas stove.

"I've been a bad girl, Sudie," said Johnsy. "Something has made that last leaf stay there to show me how wicked I was. It is a sin to want to die. You may bring me a little broth now, and some milk with a little port in it, and—no; bring me a hand-mirror first, and then pack some pillows about me, and I will sit up and watch you cook."

An hour later she said.

"Sudie, some day I hope to paint the Bay of Naples."

The doctor came in the afternoon, and Sue had an excuse to go into the hallway as he left.

"Even chances," said the doctor, taking Sue's thin, shaking hand in his. "With good nursing you'll win. And now I must see another case I have downstairs. Behrman, his name is—some kind of an artist, I believe. Pneumonia, too. He is an old, weak man, and the attack is acute. There is no hope for him; but he goes to the hospital to-day to be made more comfortable."

The next day the doctor said to Sue: "She's out of danger. You've won. Nutrition and care now—that's all."

And that afternoon Sue came to the bed where Johnsy lay,

contentedly knitting a very blue and very useless woolen shoulder scarf, and put one arm around her, pillows and all.

"I have something to tell you, white mouse," she said. "Mr. Behrman died of pneumonia to-day in the hospital. He was ill only two days. The janitor found him on the morning of the first day in his room downstairs helpless with pain. His shoes and clothing were wet through and icy cold. They couldn't imagine where he had been on such a dreadful night. And then they found a lantern, still lighted, and a ladder that had been dragged from its place, and some scattered brushes, and a palette with green and yellow colors mixed on it, and—look out the window, dear, at the last ivy leaf on the wall. Didn't you wonder why it never fluttered or moved when the wind blew? Ah, darling, it's Behrman's masterpiece—he painted it there the night that the last leaf fell."

"CHAPTER AND VERSE"

by Jeffery Deaver
Copyright © Jeffery Deaver
From his collection *More Twisted*. Used by permission of the
author

"Reverend . . . can I call you 'Reverend'?"

The round, middle-aged man in the clerical collar smiled.
"That works for me."

"I'm Detective Mike Silverman with the County Sheriff's
Department."

Reverend Stanley Lansing nodded and examined the ID and
badge that the nervously slim, salt-and-pepper—haired detective offered.

"Is something wrong?"

"Nothing involving you, sir. Not directly, I mean. Just
hoping you might be able to help us with a situation we have."

"Situation. Hmm. Well, come on inside, please, Officer . . ."

The men walked into the office connected to the First Pres-
byterian Church of Bedford, a quaint, white house of worship

that Silverman had passed a thousand times on his route between office and home and never really thought about.

That is, not until the murder this morning.

Reverend Lansing's office was musty and a gauze of dust covered most of the furniture. He seemed embarrassed. "Have to apologize. My wife and I've been away on vacation for the past week. She's still up at the lake. I came back to write my sermon — and to deliver it to my flock this Sunday, of course." He gave a wry laugh. "*If* there's anybody in the pews. Funny how religious commitment seems to go up around Christmas and then dip around vacation time." Then the man of the cloth looked around the office with a frown. "And I'm afraid I don't have anything to offer you. The church secretary's off too. Although between you and me, you're better off not sampling her coffee."

"No, I'm fine," Silverman said.

"So, what can I do for you, Officer?"

"I won't keep you long. I need some religious expertise on a case we're running. I would've gone to my father's rabbi but my question's got to do with the New Testament. That's your baili-wick, right? More than ours."

"Well," the friendly, gray-haired reverend said, wiping his glasses on his jacket lapel and replacing them, "I'm just a small-town pastor, hardly an expert. But I probably know Matthew, Mark, Luke and John better than your average rabbi, I suspect. Now, tell me how I can help."

"You've heard about the witness protection program, right?"

"Like *Goodfellas,* that sort of thing? *The Sopranos.*"

"More or less, yep. The U.S. Marshals run the federal program but we have our own state witness protection system."

"Really? I didn't know that. But I guess it makes sense."

"I'm in charge of the program in the county here and one of the people we're protecting is about to appear as a witness in a trial in Hamilton. It's our job to keep him safe through the trial and after we get a conviction—we hope—then we'll get him a new identity and move him out of the state."

"A Mafia trial?"

"Something like that."

Silverman couldn't go into the exact details of the case—how the witness, Randall Pease, a minder for drug dealer Tommy Doyle, had seen his boss put a bullet into the brain of a rival. Despite Doyle's reputation for ruthlessly murdering anyone who was a threat to him, Pease agreed to testify for a reduced sentence on assault, drug and gun charges. The state prosecutor shipped Pease off to Silverman's jurisdiction, a hundred miles from Hamilton, to keep him safe; rumor was that Doyle would do anything, pay any money, to kill his former underling—since Pease's testimony could get him the death penalty or put him away for life. Silverman had stashed the witness in a safe house near the Sheriff's Department and put a round-the-clock guard on him. The detective gave the reverend a generic description of what had happened, not mentioning names, and then said, "But there's been a setback. We had a CI —a confidential informant—"

"That's a snitch, right?"

Silverman laughed.

"I learned that from *Law and Order.* I watch it every chance I get. *CSI* too. I love cop shows." He frowned. "You mind If I say 'cop'?"

"Works for me . . . . Anyway, the informant got solid information that a professional killer's been hired to murder our witness before the trial next week."

"A hit man?"

"Yep."

"Oh, my." The reverend frowned as he touched his neck and

rubbed it near the stiff white clerical collar, where it seemed to chafe.

"But the bad guys made the snitch—found out about him, I mean—and had him killed before he could give us the details about who the hit man is and how he planned to kill my witness."

"Oh, I'm so sorry," the reverend said sympathetically. "I'll say a prayer for the man."

Silverman grunted anemic thanks but his true thoughts were that the scurvy little snitch deserved an express-lane ride to hell—not only for being a loser punk addict, but for dying before he could give the detective the particulars about the potential hit on Pease. Detective Mike Silverman didn't share with the minister that he himself had been in trouble lately in the Sheriff's Department and had been shipped off to Siberia —witness protection—because he hadn't closed any major cases in a while. He needed to make sure this assignment went smoothly, and he absolutely could not let Pease get killed.

The detective continued, "Here's where you come in—I hope. When the informant was stabbed, he didn't die right away. He managed to write a note—about a Bible passage. We think it was a clue as to how the hit man was going to kill our witness. But it's like a puzzle. We can't figure it out."

The reverend seemed intrigued. "Something from the New Testament, you said?"

"Yep," Silverman said. He opened his notebook. "The note said, 'He's on his way. Look out.' Then he wrote a chapter and verse from the Bible. We think he was going to write something else but he didn't get a chance. He was Catholic so we figure he knew the Bible pretty well— and knew something in particular in that passage that'd tell us how the hit man's going to come after our witness."

The reverend turned around and looked for a Bible on his shelf. Finally he located one and flipped it open. "What verse?"

"Luke, twelve, fifteen."

The minister found the passage and read. "Then to the people he said, 'Beware! Be on your guard against greed of every kind, for even when someone has more than enough, his possessions do not give him life.' "

"My partner brought a Bible from home. He's Christian, but he's not real religious, not a Bible-thumper . . . . Oh, hey, no offense."

"None taken. We're Presbyterians. We don't thump."

Silverman smiled. "He didn't have any idea of what that might mean. I got to thinking about your church—it's the closest one to the station house—so I thought I'd stop by and see if you can help us out. Is there anything in there you can see that'd suggest how the defendant might try to kill our witness?"

The reverend read some more from the tissue-thin pages. "This section is in one of the Gospels—where different disciples tell the story of Jesus. In chapter twelve of Luke, Jesus is warning the people about the Pharisees, urging them not to live a sinful life."

"Who were they exactly, the Pharisees?"

"They were a religious sect. In essence they believed that God existed to serve them, not the other way around. They felt they were better than everyone else and put people down. Well, that was the story back then—you never know, of course, if it's accurate. People did just as much political spinning then as they do now." Reverend Lansing tried to turn on the desk lamp but it didn't work. He fiddled with the curtains, finally opening them and letting more light into the murky office. He read the passage several times more, squinting in concentration, nodding. Silverman looked around the dim place. Books mostly. It seemed more like a professor's study than a church office. No pictures or anything else personal. You'd think even a minister would have pictures of family on his desk or walls.

Finally the man looked up. "So far, nothing really jumps out at me." He seemed frustrated.

Silverman felt the same way. Ever since the CI had been found stabbed to death that morning, the detective had been wrestling with the words from the gospel according to Luke, trying to decipher the meaning.

Beware! . . .

Reverend Lansing continued, "But I have to say, I'm fascinated with the idea. It's just like *The Da Vinci Code.* You read it?"

"No."

"It was great fun. All about secret codes and hidden messages. Say, if it's okay with you, Detective, I'd like to spend some time researching, doing some thinking about this. I love puzzles."

"I'd appreciate it, Reverend."

"I'll do what I can. You have that man under pretty good guard, I assume?"

"Oh, you bet, but it'll be risky getting him to court. We've got to figure out how the hit man's going to come at him."

"And the sooner the better, I assume."

"Yessir."

"I'll get right to it."

Grateful for the man's willingness to help, but discouraged he had no quick answers, Silverman walked out through the silent, deserted church. He climbed into his car and drove to the safe house, checked on Ray Pease. The witness was his typical obnoxious self, complaining constantly, but the officer babysitting him reported that there'd been no sign of any threats around the safe house. The detective then returned to the department.

In his office Silverman made a few calls to see if any of his other CIs had heard about the hired killer; they hadn't. His eyes kept returning to the passage, taped up on the wall in front of his desk.

"Beware! Be on your guard against greed of every kind, for even when someone has more than enough, his possessions do not give him life."

A voice startled him. "Wanta get some lunch?"

He looked up to find his partner, Steve Noveski, standing in the doorway. The junior detective, with a pleasant, round baby face, was staring obviously at his watch.

Silverman, still lost in the mysterious Bible passage, just stared at him.

"Lunch, dude," Noveski repeated. "I'm starving."

"Naw, I've gotta get this figured out." He tapped the Bible. "I'm kind of obsessed with it."

"Like, you think?" the other detective said, packing as much sarcasm into his voice as would fit.

•

That night Silverman returned home and sat distractedly through dinner with his family. His widower father had joined them, and the old man wasn't pleased that his son was so preoccupied.

"And what's that you're reading that's so important? The New Testament?" The man nodded toward the Bible he'd seen his son poring over before dinner. He shook his head and turned to his daughter-in-law. "The boy hasn't been to temple in years and he couldn't find the Pentateuch his mother and I gave him if his life depended on it. Now look, he's reading about Jesus Christ. What a son."

"It's for a case, Dad," Silverman said. "Listen, I've got some work to do. I'll see you guys later. Sorry."

"See you later sorry?" the man muttered. "And you say 'you guys' to your wife? Don't you have any respect—"

Silverman closed the door to his den, sat down at his desk and checked messages. The forensic scientist testing the murdered CI's note about the Bible passage had called to report there was no significant evidence to be found on the sheet and neither the paper nor the ink were traceable. A handwriting comparison suggested that it had been written by the victim but he couldn't be one hundred percent certain.

And, as the hours passed, there was still no word from Reverend Lansing. Sighing, Silverman stretched and stared at the words once again.

"Beware! Be on your guard against greed of every kind, for even when someone has more than enough, his possessions do not give him life."

He grew angry. A man died leaving these words to warn them. What was he trying to say?

Silverman had a vague memory of his father saying good-bye that night and later still an even more vague memory of his wife saying good night, the den door closing abruptly. She was mad. But Michael Silverman didn't care. All that mattered at the moment was finding the meaning to the message.

Something the reverend had said that afternoon came back to him. *The Da Vinci Code*. A code . . . Silverman thought about the snitch: The man hadn't been a college grad but he was smart in his own way. Maybe he had more in mind than the literal meaning of the passage; could it be that the specifics of his warning were somehow encoded in the letters themselves?

It was close to four a.m. but Silverman ignored his exhaustion and went online. He found a website about word games and puzzles. In one game you made as many words as you could out of the first letters from a saying or quotation. Okay, this could be it, Silverman thought excitedly. He wrote down the first letters of each of the words from Luke 12:15 and began rearranging them.

He got several names: *Bob, Tom, Don* . . . and dozens of words: *Gone, pen, gap* . . .

Well, *Tom* could refer to Tommy Doyle. But he could find no other clear meaning in the words or any combination of them.

What other codes were there he might try?

He tried an obvious one: assigning numbers to the letters, A equaled 1, B 2 and so on. But when he applied the formula all he ended up with were sheets of hundreds of random digits. Hopeless, he thought. Like trying to guess a computer password.

Then he thought of anagrams—where the letters of a word or phrase are rearranged to make other words. After a brief search on the web he found a site with an anagram generator, a software program that let you type in a word and a few seconds later spit out all the anagrams that could be made from it.

For hours he typed in every word and combination of words in the passage and studied the results. At six a.m., utterly exhausted, Silverman was about to give up and fall into bed. But as he was arranging the printouts of the anagrams he'd downloaded, he happened to glance at one—the anagrams that the word possessions had yielded: *open, spies, session, nose, sepsis* . . .

Something rang a bell.

"Sepsis?" he wondered out loud. It sounded familiar. He looked the word up. It meant infection. Like blood poisoning.

He was confident that he was on to something and, excited, he riffled through the other sheets. He saw that "greed" incorporated "Dr."

Yes!

And the word "guard" produced "drug."

Okay, he thought in triumph. Got it!

Detective Mike Silverman celebrated his success by falling asleep in his chair.

•

He awoke an hour later, angry at the loud engine rattling nearby —until he realized the noise was his own snoring.

The detective closed his dry mouth, winced at the pain in his back and sat up. Massaging his stiff neck, he staggered upstairs to the bedroom, blinded by the sunlight pouring through the French doors.

"Are you up already?" his wife asked blearily from bed, looking at his slacks and shirt. "It's early."

"Go back to sleep," he said.

After a fast shower he dressed and sped to the office. At eight a.m. he was in his captain's office, with his partner, Steve Noveski, beside him.

"I've figured it out."

"What?" his balding, joweled superior officer asked.

Noveski glanced at his partner with a lifted eyebrow; he'd just arrived and hadn't heard Silverman's theory yet.

"The message we got from the dead CI—how Doyle's going to kill Pease."

The captain had heard about the biblical passage but hadn't put much stock in it. "So how?" he asked skeptically.

"Doctors," Silverman announced.

"Huh?"

"I think he's going to use a doctor to try to get to Pease."

"Keep going."

Silverman told him about the anagrams.

"Like crossword puzzles?"

"Sort of."

Noveski said nothing but he too seemed skeptical of the idea.

The captain screwed up his long face. "Hold on here. You're saying that here's our CI and he's got a severed jugular and he's playing *word* games?"

"Funny how the mind works, what it see, what it can figure out."

"Funny," the senior cop muttered. "Sounds a little, whatsa word, contrived, you know what I mean?"

"He had to get us the message and he had to make sure that Doyle didn't tip to the fact he'd alerted us. He had to make it, you know, subtle enough so Doyle's boys wouldn't figure out what he knew, but not so subtle that we couldn't guess."

"I don't' know."

Silverman shook his head. "I think it works." He explained that Tommy Doyle had often paid huge fees to brilliant, ruthless hit men who'd masquerade as somebody else to get close to their unsuspecting victims. Silverman speculated that the killer would buy or steal a doctor's white jacket and get a fake ID card and a stethoscope or whatever doctors carried around with them nowadays. Then a couple of Doyle's cronies would make a halfhearted attempt on Pease's life—they couldn't get close enough to kill him in the safe house, but causing injury was a possibility. "Maybe food poisoning." Silverman explained about the sepsis anagram. "Or maybe they'd arrange for a fire or gas leak or something. The hit man, disguised as a med tech, would be allowed inside and kill Pease there. Or maybe the witness would be rushed to the hospital and the man'd cap him in the emergency room."

The captain shrugged. "Well, you can check it out—

provided you don't ignore the grunt work. We can't afford to screw this one up. We lose Pease and it's our ass."

The pronouns in those sentences may have been the first person plural but all Silverman heard was a very singular "you" and "your."

"Fair enough."

In the hallway on their way back to his office Silverman asked his partner, "Who do we have on call for medical attention at the safe house?"

"I don't know, a team from Forest Hills Hospital, I'd guess."

"We don't know who?" Silverman snapped.

"I don't, no."

"Well, find out! Then get on the horn to the safe house and tell the babysitter if Pease gets sick for any reason, needs any medicine, needs a bandage, to call me right away. Do not let any medical people see him unless we have a positive ID and I give my personal okay."

"Right."

"Then call the supervisor at Forest Hills and tell him to let me know stat if any doctors or ambulance attendants or nurses —*anybody*—don't show up for work or call in sick or if there're some doctors around that he doesn't recognize."

The young man peeled off into his office to do what Silverman had ordered and the senior detective returned to his own desk. He called a counterpart at the county sheriff's office in Hamilton and told him what he suspected and added that they had to be on the lookout for any medical people who were close to Pease.

The detective then sat back in his chair, rubbing his eyes and massaging his neck. He was more and more convinced he was right, that the secret message left by the dying informant was pointing toward a killer masquerading as a health care worker. He picked up the phone again. For several hours, he nagged hospitals and ambulance services around the county to find out if all of their people and vehicles were accounted for.

As the hour neared lunchtime, his phone rang.

"Hello?"

"Silverman." The captain's abrupt voice instantly killed the detective's sleep-deprivation haze; he was instantly alert. "We just had an attempt on Pease."

Silverman's heart thudded. He sat forward. "He okay?"

"Yeah. Somebody in an SUV fired thirty, forty shots through the front windows of the safe house. Steel-jacketed rounds, so they got through the armored glass. Pease and his guard got hit with some splinters, but nothing serious. Normally we'd send 'em to the hospital but I was thinking about what you said, about the killer pretending to be a tech or doctor, so I thought it was better to bring Pease straight here, to Detention. I'll have our sawbones look 'em both over."

"Good."

"We'll keep him here for a day or two and then send him up to the federal WP facility in Ronanka Falls."

"And have somebody head over to the Forest Hills emergency room and check out the doctors. Doyle's hired gun might be thinking we'd send him there and be waiting."

"Already ordered," the captain said.

"When'll Pease get here?"

"Anytime now."

"I'll have the lockup cleared." He hung up, rubbed his eyes again. How the hell had Doyle found out the location of the safe house? It was the best-kept secret in the department. Still, since no one had been seriously injured in the attack, he allowed himself another figurative pat of self-congratulations. His theory was being borne out. The shooter hadn't tried to kill Pease at all, just shake him up and cause enough carnage to have him dive to the floor and scrape an elbow or get cut by flying glass. Then off to the ER—and straight into the arms of Doyle's hit man.

He called the Detention supervisor at the jail and arranged to have the existing prisoners in the holding cell moved temporarily to the town police station, then told the man to brief the guards and warn them to make absolutely certain they recognized the doctor who was going to look over Pease and his bodyguard.

"I already did that. 'Causa what the captain said, you know."

Silverman was about to hang up when he glanced at the clock. It was noon, the start of second guard shift. "Did you tell the afternoon-shift personnel about the situation?"

"Oh. Forgot. I'll do it now."

Silverman hung up angrily. Did he have to think of everything himself?

He was walking to his door, headed for the Detention Center intake area to meet Pease and his guard, when his phone buzzed. The desk sergeant told him he had a visitor. "It's Reverend Lansing. He said it's urgent that he sees you. He said to tell you that he's figured out the message. You'd know what he means."

"I'll be right there."

Silverman grimaced. As soon as he'd figured out what the passage meant that morning the detective had planned to call the minister and tell him they didn't need his help any longer. But he'd forgotten all about it . . . . Well, he'd do something nice for the guy—maybe donate some money to the church or take the reverend out to lunch to thank him. Yeah, lunch would be good. They could talk about TV cop shows.

The detective met Reverend Lansing at the front desk. Silverman greeted him with a wince, noticing how exhausted he looked. "You get any sleep last night?"

The minister laughed. "Nope. Just like you, looks like."

"Come on with me, Reverend. Tell me what you came up with." He led the man down the corridor toward intake. He decided he'd hear what the man had to say. Couldn't hurt.

"I think I've got the answer to the message."

"Go on."

"Well, I was thinking that we shouldn't limit ourselves just to the verse fifteen itself. That one's just a sort of introduction to the parable that follows. I think that's the answer."

Silverman nodded, recalling what he'd read in Noveski's Bible. "The parable about the farmer?"

"Exactly. Jesus tells about a rich farmer who has a good harvest. He doesn't know what to do with the excess grain. He thinks he'll build bigger barns and figures he'll spend the rest of his life enjoying what he's done. But what happens is that God strikes him down because he's greedy. He's materially rich but spiritually impoverished."

"Okay," Silverman said. He didn't see any obvious message yet.

The reverend sensed the cop's confusion. "The point of the passage is greed. And I think that might be the key to what that poor man was trying to tell you."

They got to the intake dock and joined an armed guard who was awaiting the arrival of the armored van carrying Pease. The existing prisoners in the lockup, Silverman learned, weren't all in the transport bus yet for the transfer to the city jail.

"Tell 'em to step on it," Silverman ordered and turned back to the minister, who continued his explanation.

"So I asked myself, what's greed nowadays? And I figured it was Enron, Tyco, CEOs, internet moguls . . . . And Cahill Industries."

Silverman nodded slowly. Robert Cahill was the former head of a huge agri-business complex. After selling that company he'd turned to real estate and had put up dozens of buildings in the county. The man had just been indicted for tax evasion and insider trading.

"Successful farmer," Silverman mused. "Has a big windfall and gets in trouble. Sure. Just like the parable."

"It gets better," the minister said excitedly. "There was an editorial in the paper a few weeks ago—I tried to find it but couldn't—about Cahill. I think the editor cited a couple of Bible passages about greed. I can't remember which but I'll bet one of them was Luke twelve, fifteen."

Standing on the intake loading dock, Silverman watched the van carrying Randy Pease arrive. The detective and the guard looked around them carefully for any signs of threats as the armored vehicle backed in. Everything seemed clear. The detective knocked on the back door, and the witness and his bodyguard hurried out onto the intake loading dock. The van pulled away.

Pease started complaining immediately. He had a small cut on his forehead and a bruise on his cheek from the attack at the safe house but he moaned as if he'd fallen down a two-story flight of stairs. "I want a doctor. Look at this cut. It's already infected, I can tell. And my shoulder is killing me. What's a man gotta do to get treated right around here?"

Cops grow very talented at ignoring difficult suspects and witnesses, and Silverman hardly heard a word of the man's whiny voice.

"Cahill," Silverman said, turning back to the minister. "And what do you think that means for us?"

"Cahill owns high-rises all over town. I was wondering if the way you're going to drive your witness to the courthouse would go past any of them."

"Could be."

"So a sniper could be on top of one of them." The reverend

smiled. "I didn't actually think that up on my own. I saw it in a TV show once."

A chill went through Silverman's spine.

Sniper?

He lifted his eyes from the alley. A hundred yards away was a high-rise from whose roof a sniper would have a perfect shot into the intake loading dock where Silverman, the minister, Pease and the two guards now stood. It could very well be a Cahill building.

"Inside!" he shouted. "Now."

They all hurried into the corridor that led to the lockup and Pease's babysitter slammed the door behind them. Heart pounding from the possible near miss, Silverman picked up a phone at the desk and called the captain. He told the man the reverend's theory. The captain said, "Sure, I get it. They shoot up the safe house to flush Pease, figuring they'd bring him here and then put a shooter on the high-rise. I'll send a tactical team to scout it. Hey, bring that minister by when you've got Pease locked down. Whether he's right or not, I want to thank him."

"Will do." The detective was miffed that the brass seemed to like this idea better than the anagrams, but Silverman'd accept any theory as long as it meant keeping Pease alive.

As they waited in the dim corridor for the lockup to empty out, skinny, stringy-haired Pease began complaining again, droning on and on. "You mean there was a shooter out there and you didn't know about it, for Christ's sake, oh, sorry about the language, Father. Listen, I'm not a suspect, I'm the *star* of this show, without me—"

"Shut the hell up," Silverman snarled.

"You can't talk to me—"

Silverman's cell phone rang and he stepped away from the others to take the call. "'Lo?"

"Thank God you picked up." Steve Noveski's voice was breathless. "Where's Pease?"

"He's right in front of me," Silverman told his partner. "He's okay. There's a tac team looking for shooters in the building up the street. What's up?"

"Where's that reverend?" Noveski said. "The desk log doesn't show him signing out."

"Here, with me."

"Listen, Mike, I was thinking—what if the CI didn't leave that message from the Bible."

"Then who did?"

"What if it was the hit man himself? The one Doyle hired?"

"The killer? Why would he leave a clue?"

"It's not a clue. Think about it. He wrote the biblical stuff himself and left it near the body, as *if* the CI had left it. The killer'd figure we'd try to find a minister to help us figure it out —but not just any minister, the one at the church that's nearest the police station."

Silverman's thoughts raced to a logical conclusion. Doyle's hit man kills the minister and his wife at their summer place on the lake and masquerades as the reverend. The detective recalled that the church office had nothing in it that might identify the minister. In fact, he seemed to remember that the man had trouble even finding a Bible and didn't seem to know his desk lamp bulb was burned out. In fact, the whole church was deserted and dusty.

He continued the logical progression of events: Doyle's boys shoot up the safe house and we bring Pease here for safekeeping at the same time the reverend shows up with some story about greed and a real estate developer and a sniper— just to get close to Silverman . . . and to Pease!

He understood suddenly: There was no secret message. *He's on his way. Look out—Luke 12: 15.* It was meaningless. The killer could've written any biblical passage on the note. The whole point was to have the police contact the phony reverend and give the man access to the lockup at the same time that Pease was there.

And *I* led him right to his victim!

Dropping the phone and pulling his gun from its holster, Silverman raced up the hall and tackled the reverend. The man cried out in pain and gasped as the fall knocked the wind from his lungs. The detective pushed his gun into the hit man's neck. "Don't move a muscle."

"What're you doing?"

"What's wrong?" Pease's guard asked.

"He's the killer! He's one of Doyle's men!"

"No, I'm not. This is crazy!"

Silverman cuffed the fake minister roughly and holstered his gun. He frisked him and didn't find any weapons but figured he'd probably intended to grab one of the cops' own guns to kill Pease— and the rest of them.

The detective yanked the minister to his feet and handed him off to the intake guard. He ordered, "Take him to an interrogation room. I'll be there in ten minutes. Make sure he's shackled."

"Yessir."

"You can't do this!" the reverend shouted as he was led away roughly. "You're making a big mistake."

"Get him out of here," Silverman snapped.

Pease eyed the detective contemptuously. "He coulda killed me."

Another guard ran up the corridor from intake. "Problem, Detective?"

"We've got everything under control. But see if the lockup's empty yet. I want that man inside ASAP!" Nodding toward Pease.

"Yessir," the guard said and hurried to the intercom beside the security door leading to the cells.

Silverman looked back down the corridor, watching the minister and his escort disappear through a doorway. The detective's hands were shaking. Man, that was a close one. But at least the witness is safe.

And so is my job.

Still have to answer a hell of a lot of questions, sure, but—

"No!" a voice cried behind him. A sharp sound, like an axe in a tree trunk, resounded in the corridor, then a second, accompanied by the acrid smell of burnt gunpowder.

The detective spun around, gasping. He found himself staring in shock at the intake guard who'd just joined them. The young man held an automatic pistol mounted with a silencer and eh was standing over the bodies of the men he'd just killed: Ray Pease and the cop who'd been beside him.

Silverman reached for his own gun.

But Doyle's hit man, wearing a perfect replica of a Detention Center guard's uniform, turned his pistol on the detective and shook his head. In despair Silverman realized that he'd been partly right. Doyle's people had shot up the safe house to flush out Pease—but not to send him to the hospital; they knew the cops would bring him to the jail for safekeeping.

The hit man looked up the corridor. None of the other guards had heard or otherwise noticed the killings. The man pulled a radio from his pocket with his left hand, pushed a button and said, "It's done. Ready for the pickup."

"Good," came the tinny reply. "Right on schedule. We'll meet you in front of the station."

"Got it." He put the radio away.

Silverman opened his mouth to plead with the killer to spare his life.

But he fell silent, then gave a faint, despairing laugh as he glanced at the killer's name badge and he realized the truth—that the dead snitch's message hadn't been to mysterious after all. The CI was simply telling them to look out for a hit man masquerading as a guard whose first name was what Silverman now gaped at on the man's plastic plate: "Luke."

And, as for the chapter and verse, well, that was pretty simple too. The CI's not meant that the killer was planning the hit shortly after the start of the second shift, to give himself fifteen minutes to find where the prisoner was being held.

Right on schedule . . .

The time on the wall clock was exactly 12:15.

"COMMON DENOMINATOR"

by John D. MacDonald
(Public Domain. Appeared in *Galaxy Science Fiction,* July, 1951)

When Scout Group Forty flickered back across half the Galaxy with a complete culture study of a Class Seven civilization on three planets of Argus Ten, the Bureau of Stellar Defense had, of course, a priority claim on all data. Class Sevens were rare and of high potential danger, so all personnel of Group Forty were placed in tight quarantine during the thirty days required for a detailed analysis of the thousands of film spools.

News of the contact leaked out and professional alarmists predicted dire things on the news screens of the three home planets of Sol. A retired admiral of the Space Navy published an article in which he stated bitterly that the fleet had been weakened by twenty years of softness in high places.

On the thirty-first day, B.S.D. reported to System President Mize that the inhabitants of the three planets of Argus 10 constituted no threat, that there was no military necessity for alarm, that approval of a commerce treaty was recommended, that all data was being turned over to the Bureau of Stellar Trade and Economy for analysis, that personnel of Scout Group Forty was being given sixty days' leave before reassignment.

B.S.T.E. released film to all commercial networks at once, and visions of slavering oily monsters disappeared from the imagination of mankind. The Argonauts, as they came to be called, were pleasantly similar to mankind. It was additional proof that only in the rarest instance was the life-apex on any planet in the home Galaxy an abrupt divergence from the "human" form. The homogeneousness of planet elements throughout the Galaxy made homogeneousness of life-apex almost a truism. The bipedal, oxygen-breathing vertebrate with opposing thumb seems best suited for survival.

If was evident that, with training, the average Argonaut could pass almost unnoticed in the Solar System. The flesh tones were brightly pink, like that of a sunburned human. Cranial hair was uniformly taffy-yellow. They were heavier and more fleshy than humans. Their women had a pronounced Rubens look, a warm, moist, rosy, comfortable look.

Everyone remarked on the placidity and contentment of facial expressions, by human standards. The inevitable comparison was made. The Argonauts looked like a race of inn and beer-garden proprietors in the Bavarian Alps. With leather pants to slap, stein lids to click, feathers in Tyrolean hats and peasant skirts on their women, they would represent a culture and a way of life that had been missing from Earth for far too many generations.

Eight months after matters had been turned over to B.S.T.E., the First Trade Group returned to Earth with a bewildering variety of artifacts and devices, plus a round dozen Argonauts. The Argonauts had learned to speak Solian with an amusing guttural accent. They beamed on everything and everybody. They were great pets until the novelty wore off.

Profitable trade was inaugurated, because the Argonaut devices all seemed designed to make life more pleasant. The scent-thesizer became very popular once it was adjusted to meet human tastes. Worn as a lapel button, it could create the odor of pine, broiled steak, spring flowers, Scotch whisky, musk—even skunk for the practical jokers who exist in all ages and eras.

Any home equipped with an Argonaut static-clean never became dusty. It used no power and had to be emptied only once a year.

Technicians altered the Argonaut mechanical game animal so that it looked like an Earth rabbit. The weapons which shot a harmless beam were altered to look like rifles. After one experience with the new game, hunters were almost breathless with excitement. The incredible agility of the mechanical animal, its ability to take cover, the fact that, once the beam felled it, you could use it over and over again—all this made for the promulgation of new non-lethal hunting.

Lambert, chief of the Bureau of Racial Maturity, waited patiently for his chance at the Argonaut data. The cramped offices in the temporary wing of the old System Security Building, the meager appropriation, the obsolete office equipment, the inadequate staff all testified not only to the Bureau's lack of priority, but also to a lack of knowledge of its existence on the part of many System officials. Lambert, crag-faced, sandy, slow-moving, was a historian, anthropologist and sociologist. He was realist enough to understand that if the Bureau of Racial Maturity happened to be more important in System Government, it would probably be headed by a man with fewer academic and more political qualifications.

And Lambert knew, beyond any doubt at all, that the B.R.M. was more important to the race and the future of the race than any other branch of System Government.

Set up by President Tolles, an adult and enlightened administrator, the Bureau was now slowly being strangled by a constantly decreasing appropriation.

Lambert knew that mankind had come too far, too fast. Mankind had dropped out of a tree with all the primordial instincts to rend and tear and claw. Twenty thousand years later, and with only a few thousand years of dubiously recorded history, he had reached the stars. It was too quick.

Lambert knew that mankind must become mature in order to survive. The domination of instinct had to be watered down, and rapidly. Selective breeding might do it, but it was an answer impossible to enforce. He hoped that one day the records of an alien civilization would give him the answer. After a year of bureaucratic wriggling, feints and counter-feints, he had acquired the right of access to Scout Group Data.

As his patience dwindled he wrote increasingly firm letters to Central Files and Routing. In the end, when he finally located the data improperly stored in the closed files of the B.S.T.E., he took no more chances. He went in person with an assistant named Cooper and a commandeered electric hand-truck, and bullied a B.S.T.E. storage clerk into accepting a receipt for the Argonaut data. The clerk's cooperation was lessened by never having heard of the Bureau of Racial Maturity.

The file contained the dictionary and grammar compiled by the Scout Group, plus all the films taken on the three planets of Argus 10, plus micro-films of twelve thousand books written in the language of the Argonauts. Their written language was ideographic, and thus presented more than usual difficulties. Lambert knew that translations had been made, but somewhere along the line they had disappeared.

Lambert set his whole staff to work on the language. He hired additional linguists out of his own thin enough pocket. He gave up all outside activities in order to hasten the progress of his own knowledge. His wife, respecting Lambert's high order of devotion to his work, kept their two half-grown children from interfering during those long evenings when he studied and translated at home.

Two evenings a week Lambert called on Vonk Poogla, the Argonaut assigned to Trade Coordination, and improved his conversational Argonian to the point where he could obtain additional historical information from the pink wide "man."

Of the twelve thousand books, the number of special interest to Lambert were only one hundred and ten. On those he based his master chart. An animated film of the chart was prepared at Lambert's own expense, and, when it was done, he requested an appointment with Simpkin, Secretary for Stellar Affairs, going through all the normal channels to obtain the interview. He asked an hour of Simpkin's time. It took two weeks.

Simpkin was a big florid man with iron-gray hair, skeptical eyes and that indefinable look of political opportunism.

He came around his big desk to shake Lambert's hand. "Ah ... Lambert! Glad to see you, fella. I ought to get around to my Bureau Chiefs more often, but you know how hectic things are up here."

"I know, Mr. Secretary. I have something here of the utmost importance and—"

"Bureau of Racial Maturity, isn't it? I never did know exactly what you people do. Sort of progress records or something?"

"Of the utmost importance," Lambert repeated doggedly.

Simpkin smiled. "I hear that all day, but go ahead."

"I want to show you a chart. A historical chart of the Argonaut civilization." Lambert put the projector in position and plugged it in. He focused it on the wall screen.

"It was decided," Simpkin said firmly, "that the Argonauts are not a menace to us in any—"

"I know that, sir. Please look at the chart first and then, when you've seen it, I think you'll know what I mean."

"Go ahead," Simpkin agreed resignedly.

"I can be accused of adding apples and lemons in this presentation, sir. Note the blank chart. The base line is in years, adjusted to our calendar so as to give a comparison. Their recorded history covers twelve thousand of our years. That's better than four times ours. Now note the red line. That shows the percentage of their total population involved in wars. It peaked eight thousand years ago. Note how suddenly it drops after that. In five hundred years it sinks to the base line and does not appear again.

"Here comes the second line. Crimes of violence. It also peaks eight thousand years ago. It drops less quickly than the war line, and never does actually cut the base line. Some crime still exists there. But a very, very tiny percentage compared to ours on a population basis, or to their own past. The third line, the yellow line climbing abruptly, is the index of insanity. Again a peak during the same approximate period in their history. Again a drop almost to the base line."

Simpkin pursed his heavy lips. "Odd, isn't it?"

"Now this fourth line needs some explaining. I winnowed out death rates by age groups. Their life span is 1.3 times ours, so it had to be adjusted. I found a strange thing. I took the age group conforming to our 18 to 24 year group. That green line. Note that by the time we start getting decent figures, nine thousand years ago, it remains almost constant, and at a level conforming to our own experience. Now note what happens when the green line reaches a point eight thousand years ago. See how it begins to climb? Now steeper, almost vertical. It remains at a high level for almost a thousand years, way beyond the end of their history of war, and then descends slowly toward the base line, leveling out about two thousand years ago."

Lambert clicked off the projector.

"Is that all?" Simpkin asked.

"Isn't it enough? I'm concerned with the future of our own race. Somehow the Argonauts have found an answer to war, insanity, violence. We need that answer if we are to survive."

"Come now, Lambert," Simpkin said wearily.

"Don't you see it? Their history parallels ours. They had our same problems. They saw disaster ahead and did something about it. What did they do? I have to know that."

"How do you expect to?"

"I want travel orders to go there."

"I'm afraid that's quite impossible. There are no funds for that sort of jaunt, Lambert. And I think you are worrying over nothing."

"Shall I show you some of our own trends? Shall I show you murder turning from the most horrid crime into a relative commonplace? Shall I show you the slow inevitable increase in asylum space?"

"I know all that, man. But look at the Argonauts! Do you want that sort of stagnation? Do you want a race of fat, pink, sleepy—"

"Maybe they had a choice. A species of stagnation, or the end of their race. Faced with that choice, which would you pick, Mr. Secretary?"

"There are no funds."

"All I want is authority. I'll pay my own way."

And he did.

Rean was the home planet of the Argonauts, the third from their sun. When the trade ship flickered into three-dimensional existence, ten thousand miles above Rean, Lambert stretched the space-ache out of his long bones and muscles and smiled at Vonk Poogla.

"You could have saved me the trip, you know," Lambert said.

A grin creased the round pink visage. "Nuddink ventured, nuddink gained. Bezides, only my cousin can speak aboud this thing you vunder aboud. My cousin is werry important person. He is one picks me to go to your planet."

Vonk Poogla was transported with delight at being able to show the wonders of the ancient capital city to Lambert. It had been sacked and burned over eight thousand Earth years before, and now it was mellowed by eighty-three centuries of unbroken peace. It rested in the pastel twilight, and there were laughter and soft singing in the broad streets. Never had Lambert felt such a warm aura of security and ... love. No other word but that ultimate one seemed right.

In the morning they went to the squat blue building where Vonk Soobuknoora, the important person, had his administrative headquarters. Lambert, knowing enough of Argonaut governmental structure to understand that Soobuknoora was titular head of the three-planet government, could not help but compare the lack of protocol with what he could expect were he to try to take Vonk Poogla for an interview with President Mize.

Soobuknoora was a smaller, older edition of Poogla, his pink face wrinkled, his greening hair retaining only a trace of the original yellow. Soobuknoora spoke no Solian and he was very pleased to find that Lambert spoke Argonian.

Soobuknoora watched the animated chart with considerable interest. After it was over, he seemed lost in thought.

"It is something so private with us, Man Lambert, that we seldom speak of it to each other," Soobuknoora said in Argonian. "It is not written. Maybe we have shame—a guilt sense. That is hard to say. I have decided to tell you what took place among us eight thousand years ago."

"I would be grateful."

"We live in contentment. Maybe it is good, maybe it is not

so good. But we continue to live. Where did our trouble come from in the old days, when we were like your race? Back when we were brash and young and wickedly cruel? From the individuals, those driven ones who were motivated to succeed despite all obstacles. They made our paintings, wrote our music, killed each other, fomented our unrest, our wars. We live off the bewildering richness of our past."

He sighed. "It was a problem. To understand our solution, you must think of an analogy, Man Lambert. Think of a factory where machines are made. We will call the acceptable machines stable, the unacceptable ones unstable. They are built with a flywheel which must turn at a certain speed. If it exceeds that speed, it is no good. But a machine that is stable can, at any time, become unstable. What is the solution?" He smiled at Lambert.

"I'm a bit confused," Lambert confessed. "You would have to go around inspecting the machines constantly for stability."

"And use a gauge? No. Too much trouble. An unstable machine can do damage. So we do this—we put a little governor on the machine. When the speed passes the safety mark, the machine breaks."

"But this is an analogy, Vonk Soobuknoora!" Lambert protested. "You can't put a governor on a man!"

"Man is born with a governor, Man Lambert. Look back in both our histories, when we were not much above the animal level. An unbalanced man would die. He could not compete for food. He could not organize the simple things of his life for survival. Man Lambert, did you ever have a fleeting impulse to kill yourself?"

Lambert smiled. "Of course. You could almost call that impulse a norm for intelligent species."

"Did it ever go far enough so that you considered a method, a weapon?"

Lambert nodded slowly. "It's hard to remember, but I think I did. Yes, once I did."

"And what would have happened," the Argonaut asked softly, "if there had been available to you in that moment a weapon completely painless, completely final?"

Lambert's mouth went dry. "I would probably have used it. I was very young. Wait! I'm beginning to see what you mean, but—"

"The governor had to be built into the body," Soobuknoora interrupted, "and yet so designed that there would be no possibility of accidental activation. Suppose that on this day I start to think of how great and powerful I am in this position I have. I get an enormous desire to become even more powerful. I begin to reason emotionally. Soon I have a setback. I am depressed. I am out of balance, you could say. I have become dangerous to myself and to our culture.

"In a moment of depression, I take these two smallest fingers of each hand. I reach behind me and I press the two fingers, held firmly together, to a space in the middle of my back. A tiny capsule buried at the base of my brain is activated and I am dead within a thousandth part of a second. Vonk Poogla is the same. All of us are the same. The passing urge for self-destruction happens to be the common denominator of imbalance. We purged our race of the influence of the neurotic, the egocentric, the hypersensitive, merely by making self-destruction very, very easy."

"Then that death rate—?"

"At eighteen the operation is performed. It is very quick and very simple. We saw destruction ahead. We had to force it through. In the beginning the deaths were frightening, there were so many of them. The stable ones survived, bred, reproduced. A lesser but still great percentage of the next generation went—and so on, until now it is almost static."

In Argonian Lambert said hotly, "Oh, it sounds fine! But what about children? What sort of heartless race can plant the seed of death in its own children?"

Never before had he seen the faintest trace of anger on any Argonaut face. The single nostril widened and Soobuknoora might have raged if he had been from Earth. "There are other choices, Man Lambert. Our children have no expectation of being burned to cinder, blown to fragments. They are free of that fear. Which is the better love, Man Lambert?"

"I have two children. I couldn't bear to—"

"Wait!" Soobuknoora said. "Think one moment. Suppose you were to know that when they reached the age of eighteen, both your children were to be operated on by our methods. How would that affect your present relationship to them?"

Lambert was, above all, a realist. He remembered the days of being "too busy" for the children, of passing off their serious questions with a joking or curt evasion, of playing with them as though they were young, pleasing, furry animals.

"I would do a better job, as a parent," Lambert admitted. "I would try to give them enough emotional stability so that they would never—have that urge to kill themselves. But Ann is delicate, moody, unpredictable, artistic."

Poogla and Soobuknoora nodded in unison. "You would probably lose that one; maybe you would lose both," Soobuknoora agreed. "But it is better to lose more than half the children of a few generations to save the race."

Lambert thought some more. He said, "I shall go back and I shall speak of this plan and what it did for you. But I do not think my race will like it. I do not want to insult you or your people, but you have stagnated. You stand still in time."

Vonk Poogla laughed largely. "Not by a damn sight," he said gleefully. "Next year we stop giving the operation. We stop for good. It was just eight thousand years to permit us to catch our breath before going on more safely. And what is eight thousand years of marking time in the history of a race? Nothing, my friend. Nothing!"

When Lambert went back to Earth, he naturally quit his job.

"MADDENED BY MYSTERY: OR, THE DEFECTIVE DETECTIVE"

by Steven Leacock
(Public Domain)

The great detective sat in his office. He wore a long green gown and half a dozen secret badges pinned to the outside of it.

Three or four pairs of false whiskers hung on a whisker-stand beside him.

Goggles, blue spectacles and motor glasses lay within easy reach.

He could completely disguise himself at a second's notice.

Half a bucket of cocaine and a dipper stood on a chair at his elbow.

His face was absolutely impenetrable.

A pile of cryptograms lay on the desk. The Great Detective hastily tore them open one after the other, solved them, and threw them down the cryptogram-shute at his side.

There was a rap at the door.

The Great Detective hurriedly wrapped himself in a pink

domino, adjusted a pair of false black whiskers and cried, "Come in."

His secretary entered.

"Ha," said the detective, "it is you!"

He laid aside his disguise.

"Sir," said the young man in intense excitement, "a mystery has been committed!"

"Ha!" said the Great Detective, his eye kindling, "is it such as to completely baffle the police of the entire continent?"

"They are so completely baffled with it," said the secretary, "that they are lying collapsed in heaps; many of them have committed suicide."

"So," said the detective, "and is the mystery one that is absolutely unparalleled in the whole recorded annals of the London police?"

"It is."

"And I suppose," said the detective, "that it involves names which you would scarcely dare to breathe, at least without first using some kind of atomiser or throat-gargle."

"Exactly."

"And it is connected, I presume, with the highest diplomatic consequences, so that if we fail to solve it England will be at war with the whole world in sixteen minutes?"

His secretary, still quivering with excitement, again answered yes.

"And finally," said the Great Detective, "I presume that it was committed in broad daylight, in some such place as the entrance of the Bank of England, or in the cloak-room of the House of Commons, and under the very eyes of the police?"

"Those," said the secretary, "are the very conditions of the mystery."

"Good," said the Great Detective, "now wrap yourself in

this disguise, put on these brown whiskers and tell me what it is."

The secretary wrapped himself in a blue domino with lace insertions, then, bending over, he whispered in the ear of the Great Detective:

"The Prince of Wurttemberg has been kidnapped."

The Great Detective bounded from his chair as if he had been kicked from below.

A prince stolen! Evidently a Bourbon! The scion of one of the oldest families in Europe kidnapped. Here was a mystery indeed worthy of his analytical brain.

His mind began to move like lightning.

"Stop!" he said, "how do you know this?"

The secretary handed him a telegram. It was from the Prefect of Police of Paris. It read: "The Prince of Wurttemberg stolen. Probably forwarded to London. Must have him here for the opening day of Exhibition. 1,000 pounds reward."

So! The Prince had been kidnapped out of Paris at the very time when his appearance at the International Exposition would have been a political event of the first magnitude.

With the Great Detective to think was to act, and to act was to think. Frequently he could do both together.

"Wire to Paris for a description of the Prince."

The secretary bowed and left.

At the same moment there was slight scratching at the door.

A visitor entered. He crawled stealthily on his hands and knees. A hearthrug thrown over his head and shoulders disguised his identity.

He crawled to the middle of the room.

Then he rose.

Great Heaven!

It was the Prime Minister of England.

"You!" said the detective.

"Me," said the Prime Minister.

"You have come in regard the kidnapping of the Prince of Wurttemberg?"

The Prime Minister started. "How do you know?" he said.

The Great Detective smiled his inscrutable smile.

"Yes," said the Prime Minister. "I will use no concealment. I am interested, deeply interested. Find the Prince of Wurttemberg, get him safe back to Paris and I will add 500 pounds to the reward already offered. But listen," he said impressively as he left the room, "see to it that no attempt is made to alter the marking of the prince, or to clip his tail."

So! To clip the Prince's tail! The brain of the Great Detective reeled. So! a gang of miscreants had conspired to—but no! the thing was not possible.

There was another rap at the door.

A second visitor was seen. He wormed his way in, lying almost prone upon his stomach, and wriggling across the floor. He was enveloped in a long purple cloak. He stood up and peeped over the top of it.

Great Heaven!

It was the Archbishop of Canterbury!

"Your Grace!" exclaimed the detective in amazement—"pray do not stand, I beg you. Sit down, lie down, anything rather than stand."

The Archbishop took off his mitre and laid it wearily on the whisker-stand.

"You are here in regard to the Prince of Wurttemberg."

The Archbishop started and crossed himself. Was the man a magician?

"Yes," he said, "much depends on getting him back. But I have only come to say this: my sister is desirous of seeing you. She is coming here. She has been extremely indiscreet and her fortune hangs upon the Prince. Get him back to Paris or I fear she will be ruined."

The Archbishop regained his mitre, uncrossed himself, wrapped his cloak about him, and crawled stealthily out on his hands and knees, purring like a cat.

The face of the Great Detective showed the most profound sympathy. It ran up and down in furrows. "So," he muttered, "the sister of the Archbishop, the Countess of Dashleigh!" Accustomed as he was to the life of the aristocracy, even the Great Detective felt that there was here intrigue of more than customary complexity.

There was a loud rapping at the door.

There entered the Countess of Dashleigh. She was all in furs.

She was the most beautiful woman in England. She strode imperiously into the room. She seized a chair imperiously and seated herself on it, imperial side up.

She took off her tiara of diamonds and put it on the tiara-holder beside her and uncoiled her boa of pearls and put it on the pearl-stand.

"You have come," said the Great Detective, "about the Prince of Wurttemberg."

"Wretched little pup!" said the Countess of Dashleigh in disgust.

So! A further complication! Far from being in love with the Prince, the Countess denounced the young Bourbon as a pup!

"You are interested in him, I believe."

"Interested!" said the Countess. "I should rather say so. Why, I bred him!"

"You which?" gasped the Great Detective, his usually impassive features suffused with a carmine blush.

"I bred him," said the Countess, "and I've got 10,000 pounds upon his chances, so no wonder I want him back in

Paris. Only listen," she said, "if they've got hold of the Prince and cut his tail or spoiled the markings of his stomach it would be far better to have him quietly put out of the way here."

The Great Detective reeled and leaned up against the side of the room. So! The cold-blooded admission of the beautiful woman for the moment took away his breath! Herself the mother of the young Bourbon, misallied with one of the greatest families of Europe, staking her fortune on a Royalist plot, and yet with so instinctive a knowledge of European politics as to know that any removal of the hereditary birth-marks of the Prince would forfeit for him the sympathy of the French populace.

The Countess resumed her tiara.

She left.

The secretary re-entered.

"I have three telegrams from Paris," he said, "they are completely baffling."

He handed over the first telegram.

It read:

"The Prince of Wurttemberg has a long, wet snout, broad ears, very long body, and short hind legs."

The Great Detective looked puzzled.

He read the second telegram.

"The Prince of Wurttemberg is easily recognised by his deep bark."

And then the third.

"The Prince of Wurttemberg can be recognised by a patch of white hair across the centre of his back."

The two men looked at one another. The mystery was maddening, impenetrable.

The Great Detective spoke.

"Give me my domino," he said. "These clues must be followed up," then pausing, while his quick brain analysed and summed up the evidence before him—"a young man," he muttered, "evidently young since described as a 'pup,' with a long, wet snout (ha! addicted obviously to drinking), a streak of white hair across his back (a first sign of the results of his abandoned life)—yes, yes," he continued, "with this clue I shall find him easily."

The Great Detective rose.

He wrapped himself in a long black cloak with white whiskers and blue spectacles attached.

Completely disguised, he issued forth.

He began the search.

For four days he visited every corner of London.

He entered every saloon in the city. In each of them he drank a glass of rum. In some of them he assumed the disguise of a sailor. In others he entered as a solider. Into others he penetrated as a clergyman. His disguise was perfect. Nobody paid any attention to him as long as he had the price of a drink.

The search proved fruitless.

Two young men were arrested under suspicion of being the Prince, only to be released.

The identification was incomplete in each case.

One had a long wet snout but no hair on his back.

The other had hair on his back but couldn't bark.

Neither of them was the young Bourbon.

The Great Detective continued his search.

He stopped at nothing.

Secretly, after nightfall, he visited the home of the Prime Minister. He examined it from top to bottom. He measured all the doors and windows. He took up the flooring. He inspected the plumbing. He examined the furniture. He found nothing.

With equal secrecy he penetrated into the palace of the Archbishop. He examined it from top to bottom. Disguised as a choir-boy he took part in the offices of the church. He found nothing.

Still undismayed, the Great Detective made his way into the home of the Countess of Dashleigh. Disguised as a housemaid, he entered the service of the Countess.

Then at last a clue came which gave him a solution of the mystery.

On the wall of the Countess's boudoir was a large framed engraving.

It was a portrait.

Under it was a printed legend:

THE PRINCE OF WURTTEMBERG

The portrait was that of a Dachshund.

The long body, the broad ears, the unclipped tail, the short hind legs—all was there.

In a fraction of a second the lightning mind of the Great Detective had penetrated the whole mystery.

THE PRINCE WAS A DOG!!!!

Hastily throwing a domino over his housemaid's dress, he rushed to the street. He summoned a passing hansom, and in a few moments was at his house.

"I have it," he gasped to his secretary. "The mystery is solved. I have pieced it together. By sheer analysis I have reasoned it out. Listen—hind legs, hair on back, wet snout, pup —eh, what? does that suggest nothing to you?"

"Nothing," said the secretary; "it seems perfectly hopeless."

The Great Detective, now recovered from his excitement, smiled faintly.

"It means simply this, my dear fellow. The Prince of Wurttemberg is a dog, a prize Dachshund. The Countess of Dash-leigh bred him, and he is worth some 25,000 pounds in addition to the prize of 10,000 pounds offered at the Paris dog show. Can you wonder that——"

At that moment the Great Detective was interrupted by the scream of a woman.

"Great Heaven!"

The Countess of Dashleigh dashed into the room.

Her face was wild.

Her tiara was in disorder.

Her pearls were dripping all over the place.

She wrung her hands and moaned.

"They have cut his tail," she gasped, "and taken all the hair off his back. What can I do? I am undone!!"

"Madame," said the Great Detective, calm as bronze, "do yourself up. I can save you yet."

"You!"

"Me!"

"How?"

"Listen. This is how. The Prince was to have been shown at Paris."

The Countess nodded.

"Your fortune was staked on him?"

The Countess nodded again.

"The dog was stolen, carried to London, his tail cut and his marks disfigured."

Amazed at the quiet penetration of the Great Detective, the Countess kept on nodding and nodding.

"And you are ruined?"

"I am," she gasped, and sank to the floor in a heap of pearls.

"Madame," said the Great Detective, "all is not lost."

He straightened himself up to his full height. A look of inflinchable unflexibility flickered over his features.

The honour of England, the fortune of the most beautiful woman in England was at stake.

"I will do it," he murmured.

"Rise dear lady," he continued. "Fear nothing. I WILL IMPERSONATE THE DOG!!!"

That night the Great Detective might have been seen on the deck of the Calais packet boat with his secretary. He was on his hands and knees in a long black cloak, and his secretary had him on a short chain.

He barked at the waves exultingly and licked the secretary's hand.

"What a beautiful dog," said the passengers.

The disguise was absolutely complete.

The Great Detective had been coated over with mucilage to which dog hairs had been applied. The markings on his back were perfect. His tail, adjusted with an automatic coupler, moved up and down responsive to every thought. His deep eyes were full of intelligence.

Next day he was exhibited in the Dachshund class at the International show.

He won all hearts.

"*Quel beau chien!*" cried the French people.

"*Ach! was ein Dog!*" cried the Spanish.

The Great Detective took the first prize!

The fortune of the Countess was saved.

Unfortunately as the Great Detective had neglected to pay the dog tax, he was caught and destroyed by the dog-catchers. But that is, of course, quite outside of the present narrative, and is only mentioned as an odd fact in conclusion.

8

AUTHOR'S NOTE

Thanks for reading my book. Helping writers is my passion, so please take a moment to sign up for my occasional email updates. You'll be the first to know about my book releases and special deals. My emails are short and I won't stuff your mailbox, and you can certainly unsubscribe at any time. If you do sign up, I'll put your name in the random drawing I do each month for a free book.

You can sign up by going to:

www.jamesscottbell.com

Look for the FREE BOOK page.

Also, my comprehensive training course in the craft of best-selling fiction is now available. An investment that will pay off for your entire career.

https://knockoutfiction.teachable.com/p/novel

Made in the USA
San Bernardino, CA
31 May 2019